# THE GOLDEN AGE OF COLLEGE TENNIS

$15.95

Cover Design
Kathryn Donohew

# THE GOLDEN AGE OF COLLEGE TENNIS

---

## A USC COACH'S UNIQUE INFLUENCE ON THE GAME

GEORGE TOLEY

WITH

JOE JARES

**THE AMERICAS GROUP**

The Americas Group
654 N. Sepulveda Blvd., Suite 1
Los Angeles, California 90049-2070
U.S.A.
☎ + (1) 310 476 6374
FX + (1) 310 471 3276
EM hrmg@mac.com
www.AmericasGroup.com

ISBN:
978-0-935047-64-6


Library of Congress Cataloging-in-Publication Data

Toley, George, 1923-2008.
 The golden age of college tennis : a usc coach's unique influence on the game / George Toley with Joe Jares. -- 1st ed.
     p. cm.
 Includes index.
 ISBN 978-0-935047-64-6
 1. Toley, George, 1923-2008. 2. Tennis coaches--United States--Biography. 3. Tennis players--United States--Biography. I. Jares, Joe, 1937- II. Title.

GV994.T65 2009
796.342--dc22

                                    2008048823

Printed in the United States of America
Fidlar Doubleday

# TABLE OF CONTENTS

# INTRODUCTION

I have long felt that George Toley was the best teacher and coach of tennis anywhere.

He was an excellent player in his day, competing with and against the likes of Bobby Riggs, Gardnar Mulloy, Bitsy Grant and Ellsworth Vines, but he just missed cracking the U.S. top 10. It was as a coach that he had a Hall of Fame career – in fact, he is already in the Men's Collegiate Tennis Hall of Fame (along with five of his players) for having coached 10 NCAA-championship teams at the University of Southern California. Toley also was the longtime head teaching pro at the legendary Los Angeles Tennis Club and coach of the girls at Marlborough School.

Four of his USC players, Alex Olmedo, Rafael Osuna, Dennis Ralston and Stan Smith, are in the International Tennis Hall of Fame. His athletes have won countless tournaments, and 74 of them have won at least 429 national and international titles, led by Smith (49), Raul Ramirez (30), Ralston (24), Dick Leach (22) and Sally Moore Huss (21). This does not include Davis Cup – his players have competed in 13 challenge or final rounds and at least 56 preliminary rounds. Six have served as Davis Cup captains for the United States (Ralston) or Mexico (Francisco Contreras, Eduardo Guzman, Yves Lemaitre, Eduardo Martinez Lanz, Ramirez). Five have served as Federation Cup captains for Mexico (Elena Osuna, Alejandra Vallejo, Joaquin Loyo-Mayo, Ramirez and Claudia Hernandez).

Along with being a great teacher who prepared his players with sound fundamentals, Toley had an amazing knack of telling them just what they should do to pull out victory. For example, in 1975 the NCAA Tournament was in Corpus Christi, Texas. In a second-round match, Chris Lewis, a future All-America who was then just a sophomore, trailed a man from Western Michigan 4-1 in the third set. At the changeover, Toley said, "This guy is knocking off winners on first serves, off ground strokes and is loose as a goose. I don't think he can keep it up. Stay on the baseline, push with him and I think he'll start making some errors. When the score gets to 4-4, you can play your normal game and beat him." That is exactly what happened.

The greatest tribute I ever heard paid to any coach, anywhere, was paid to Coach Toley by Lewis afterward. He told me, "Coach is a genius. He just won another match for me. It isn't fair that you guys have to compete against him."

If you put the 20 best college coaches in a room and George Toley walked in, I contend he'd know more than all 20 combined. He had no peer. Besides that, he was the most thoughtful, kind, generous and beautiful person I've ever met. Seeing him once or twice a year for many years was among my greatest pleasures.

*Stan Drobac*
Tennis Coach Emeritus
Michigan State University

East Lansing, Michigan
November 2008

Coach George Toley (1916-2008)

# BEGINNING

George Toley teaching younger players.
(Photo courtesy of the USC Sports Archives)

# BEGINNING

I was born in Los Angeles on April 23, 1916, Easter Sunday, and grew up in a neighborhood called Angelino Heights, above Sunset Boulevard and near where Dodger Stadium is now. According to the L.A. Times, "in 1983 the entire area qualified as Los Angeles' first historic district." Our house was on Everett Street, a cul de sac on a steep hill. There was a big park up there and we had 15 or 20 kids who had a ball playing in the park or on the street. It was a great boyhood.

Both of my parents, Kate and Andrew, were of Croatian descent and both were born in Yugoslavia. My dad's original surname was Tolj, but people had trouble pronouncing the name and writing it, so he changed it to Toley. My mom's maiden name was Boroya.

They met in Los Angeles, which has become the most diverse city in the world but wasn't as diverse then. Dad's job was with the Southern Pacific Railroad. Train wrecks happened frequently and his job was to go to the scene and tell the workers how to clean up the mess. He did that for a number of years. Later he went into the house-building business.

Mom was a fiend for health and one thing we always

had was soup – every meal. She grew some of the vegetables right there in our backyard. There were never canned goods in the house. She would say, "That's poison." Everything was wholesome. For instance, she made the bread after getting the flour from the Grand Central Market at Ninth and Central, where there was a store that had maybe 15 varieties of flour.

I had an older sister, Lucille, and a younger sister, Pauline. They were wonderful but not athletic at all. They were self-taught tailors and made their own clothes. I started driving when I was 12 and I would have to chauffeur them to clothing stores to buy yarn, thread and fabric. I had to be there an hour or two waiting for them to decide. They were the two best-dressed girls in school.

How I got started in tennis was because of Johnny Beradino, a kid in my homeroom at Central Junior High, which is long gone. We'd earn points for our homeroom by competing in various sports. One day John said to me, "George, they're having a doubles tournament this semester. There's a singles tournament one semester and a doubles tournament the next; let's enter the doubles."

"John, I've never played tennis in my life," I said. I was 14 or 15, in the ninth grade.*

"Hardly anybody else here plays," he said, "so let's just enter anyway."

I can't remember whether I practiced or not, but we entered the tournament and we won. Then the next semester it was singles and I won that, too.

---

\* This was a relatively late start in the sport. For comparison, Martina Navratilova began at age 4 1/2, Monica Seles at 5, Ilie Nastase at 6 or 7, Gardnar Mulloy at 11 and Arthur Ashe at 12.

Maybe Beradino should have pressed me harder to play baseball. He went on to play one season for USC and all or part of 13 seasons in the major leagues, for the St. Louis Browns, Cleveland and Pittsburgh. Or maybe he should have pressed me to join a drama class. After his baseball career, he got into acting and played Dr. Steve Hardy for more than 30 seasons in "General Hospital," one of the most famous soap operas in TV history.

In my last year at Central, there was a beautiful girl named Sarah Jane Faulks. I used to walk her home and we kissed a number of times. Like Beradino, she went into show business, becoming a dumb blonde in her first movies, then blossoming into the star of such films as "Jezebel," "Wuthering Heights," "The Yearling," "The Blue Veil," "Mrs. Miniver" and "The Best Years of Our Lives." She was nominated four times for the best-actress Oscar and won it in 1948 for "Johnny Belinda." She was known then as Jane Wyman and was the first wife of actor (later governor of California and President) Ronald Reagan.

I lived in the Belmont High School district, but I had always been a putterer and Belmont didn't have the courses I wanted. Polytechnic High, then downtown but now in the San Fernando Valley, had tremendous classes for someone who wanted to be an architect or mechanical engineer or electrical engineer. So I turned in a fake address and started at Poly, which had a forge and a foundry, a big machine shop, steam and gas, big turbine engines. People who graduated from there could get jobs immediately.

Poly had no tennis courts, no tennis team. A pal and I didn't know what sport to go out for and we finally settled on cross country. We didn't have to have any experience. We reported and that day we had to run, and he and I decided, "To hell with this." He turned out to be one of the top actors in Hollywood, Anthony Quinn.

The principal sympathized with my desire to play tennis and after about a year and a half there, he let me transfer to L.A. High. I had to sit out a year, so I played just one season for the Romans as the No. 2 in singles behind Lawrence Nelson. He was good enough to have had a victory over Bobby Riggs, who was at Franklin High at the time.

(Riggs was two years younger than me, but he was the best junior in Southern California. He was a senior in high school, or just out, when he won the national men's clay court title in 1936 and 1937.

(Some years later, I went into a paint store one day. I was in tennis clothes and one of the clerks said, "Oh, you're a tennis player." I said, "Sure." He said, "Well, I'll tell you something. I played basketball with Bobby Riggs at Franklin High. The coach always wanted to kick him off the team. He wouldn't come to practice. But the coach wouldn't kick him off because he always made All-City."

("Always made All-City" was an exaggeration, I found out. Riggs did get plaudits in an L.A. Times column for scoring 17 points in a "B" game – a lot of points for those days. And he was a superb athlete. Great Ping Pong player. Any sport, he had great athletic ability.)

After graduation in 1935, the depths of the Depression, I rented a garage behind the L.A. High tennis courts and turned it into a tennis shop. (My parents had not gone to college and didn't push me or my sisters to go.) There were the high school courts and Queen Anne Recreation Center was about a block away. We played tennis at both places and also I played some at

La Cienega Playground, which had the nicest public courts in the metropolis.

My shop was far from posh. I sold some balls and equipment and strung rackets by hand. I had strung my first racket in my kitchen, using a couple of ice picks.

My mother and my sister, Lu, came out to see me play in the final of a tournament at Griffith Park. It was a city event and I won it. After the tournament, my mother said to me, "George, would you mind if I didn't watch you anymore? I got so nervous I was sick." That was the only match my family ever saw me play.

# TOLEY'S TIPS - 1

*SERVE OR RECEIVE?*: If you win the coin toss, you usually should choose to serve first. All the professionals do. One important reason is when you're starting a match, often you're not completely warmed up. You want to make sure you win that first game and your chances of doing that are a hell of a lot better when you're serving than when you're returning.

**ARGUING CALLS:** I would tell my players, "Look, if you think that point is going to cost you the match, then you just don't have any confidence in yourself. You should feel you're going to win the match regardless of what the calls are. Go out there and let the umpires umpire and you play your tennis. If you can get a bad call and forget it, you've done a great thing toward winning the match."
It's bad for a person's concentration to argue with an umpire or linesman. (Some players feel they need to kick up a fuss to motivate themselves. For most, I don't buy it.)

*THE BACKBOARD, AN OPPONENT THAT NEVER MISSES:* It can be good practice to hit against a backboard. I've been told that the great French Davis Cup hero, Rene Lacoste, would hit against a backboard in the 10-minute rest period then allowed after the third set of a five-set match.

You can hit many more balls in a short length of time, you can do it by yourself, and you can develop a rhythm and a groove much easier than against a partner on the court (the ball doesn't come back the same way all the time with the latter). A ball machine can help the same way but is much more expensive.

*DIRECTING THE BALL:* For crosscourt shots, meet the ball about eight inches forward of the front foot. For down the line, meet the ball approximately opposite the front foot. That's on the forehand. On the backhand, for crosscourt shots, make it 12 inches forward of the front foot. For down the line, six inches forward of the front foot. The contact point must be precise.

# THE CIRCUIT AND MIAMI

### Ed Atkinson
(Photo courtesy of the USC Sports Archives)

# THE CIRCUIT AND MIAMI

I had been saving my money to go play the circuit in 1937 in the East, the clay tournaments first, and then the grass, leading up to the U.S. Championship at Forest Hills, Borough of Queens, New York City.

I had played little junior tennis, but Perry T. Jones, the big wheel of the Southern California Tennis Association, knew me. I went to see him and he turned me over to a fellow named Chuck Carr, who laid out an itinerary for me.

There was little or no money for tennis players in those days, but I was able to travel the circuit in part because I brought along a vise to help me string rackets in my room. Most players don't know how to string, or just don't want to do it.

I wouldn't string any rackets while I was still playing, because it would tighten my muscles. But as soon as I lost, players would come to me by the dozens to string. The players hounded me and I made a good amount of money because they gave me two dollars per racket, plus they paid for the gut. The gut came in two 21-inch lengths, which was more than I needed, so I would save some for the next job. My earnings per job came out to four or five dollars, which in those days was a lot of money.

I strung one racket in 20 minutes for Gene Mako, that was my fastest. (Mako won five major titles in the late 1930s.) There was a trip coming up to Canada and I had to make the train. Usually it took half an hour.

When we played, Johnson's Chrome Twist was the best gut in the world, made out of sheep intestines. I think Johnson might still be the leader in manufacturing pharmaceutical sutures. The Australians used to come to the U.S. and load up on it. Johnson didn't put any chemicals in the making of the gut to make it last longer. The strings from makers who did that lacked flexibility.

There was one fellow who played with a rubber-strung racket. Those strings just flung the ball too much; you lacked control. But you could really hit the ball hard with it. The rubber would just rebound it.

Speaking of equipment, the ball in those days, and even into the 1950s, was lighter and flightier. It went through the air much faster than the ball does today. It was easy to hit hard, favoring the server, but it was hard to control. You couldn't swat it, you had to guide it – the ball was kept on the strings much longer. Vic Braden, who has studied a lot of tennis on videotape, says it is a myth that the ball lingered longer on the strings, but it sure seemed that way to all of us at the time. Don Budge and Jack Kramer, they carried the ball more. You had to be precise to keep it in play. Because of all the topspin, guys swing their rackets today through the air twice as fast as Budge and Kramer.

The lighter ball made the game different in a lot of ways. In those years, we never aimed an overhead. All we did was bounce it over the fence. That's all we had to do, even if we were deep, back near the baseline. And most of the guys were volleyers, because with that light ball, it was hard to hit accurate passing shots.

And on grass, with new balls, it was just like heaven – you could spin it, you could hit the American twist with it, you could hit the flat ball. Back when I was playing, almost everyone had an American twist serve in his repertoire. As the ball got heavier, we couldn't do it. It was hard on our backs and the ball wouldn't take off as it had.

There was a big left-hander from Santa Monica High and Stanford, Johnny Doeg, who won the nationals only because of his serve with that lighter ball. In 1930 he beat Francis X. Shields in four sets. All he had on both sides was a chip, so he was barely adequate. Except he could serve four aces in a row. I knew him on the circuit about a decade later and he admitted, ``I never could have won the nationals if they were using the ball they're using now.''

I was never conscious of the change in the ball. It was a progressive, gradual thing, the ball getting heavier, with more fuzz on it. The companies changed the material because they were competing to make a ball that would last longer. And it made it a better game, giving the baseliner more of a chance.

My first tournament was in Cincinnati on clay, not just singles but also doubles with my friend from L.A., Bobby Riggs – not a bad way to begin. I saw that he didn't have a partner and asked him to play with me. (I had played in only one clay-court tournament, in San Diego.) In singles I got to the semis against Dr. John McDiarmid, who was ranked ninth in the nation, and lost to him in four sets. In doubles, we were playing a couple of guys from Florida in the semis. Riggs wanted to make a bet with them. He was chucking the match and kept talking to them, urging them to make a bet. They kept negative on it; they kept negative so long that finally we lost. That was Bobby.

After we won a match at that event, we were walking to the locker room and somebody handed Riggs a telegram. I said, ``What cooks?'' He said, ``Another tournament, one I'm not going to, just sent me a better offer than the one I'm going to.' I said, ``What are you going to do?'' He grinned and said, ``George, what do you think I'm going to do?'' That was Bobby, too. As I recall, we didn't play together again that summer. He usually played with Wayne Sabin.

Riggs once gave me a set at the National Clay Courts. He was that way. He wanted to stay on the court longer, I think, to practice getting back in a match and winning it from way down. He wanted the pressure of it.

Bobby didn't have power, but he had everything else – great touch and concentration and very fluent strokes. He was a pretty player to see hit the ball. People didn't realize how good his serve was. A strange thing about Bob, because of his being a steady-type player without power, you would think clay would have been his best surface. But it was not. Grass was his best surface, because it added that little power to his game that wasn't there when he was on clay. And that little extra power made a big difference. He would play someone on clay and have a long, five-set battle. Then he'd play the same man on grass and it would be over quickly. And of all the players I've ever seen, he had the best lob. With his great touch, he could put a lob within three or four inches of the baseline consistently.

At this point, at the start of the circuit in Cincinnati, I was hearing nothing from the tournaments. Jones didn't do anything to help me, so I was paying my own room and board. Riggs said, ``Well, let me call.'' He got me room and board at Louisville and $25 or so for expenses, which wasn't too bad. Took care of the week, that's for sure. For the rest of the summer, I got room and board and some expenses wherever I went.

I did fairly well. Won the doubles at Saginaw, Mich. Played on grass for the first time, at Brookline, Mass., and lost in the first round to the No. 1 player from Yale. Lost in the final of doubles. Then Seabright, N.J., Southhampton, N.Y., Rye, N.Y., Newport, R.I., and Forest Hills.

Maybe my biggest win of that summer was 8-6, 6-4, 6-1 at Forest Hills over future Hall of Famer Jacques ``Toto'' Brugnon, the oldest of France's famous Four Musketeers, who were Davis Cup heroes in the late 1920s and early 1930s. I lost to Wayne Sabin, a top-10 player, in four sets in the next round.*

I was hoping to earn a tennis scholarship. Don McNeill, who was to become NCAA singles champion at Kenyon College in 1940, said I could get a scholarship there. I visited the campus in Gambier, Ohio – it's in northeastern Ohio, south of Cleveland and west of Pittsburgh -- in snowy country. Not for me. A UCLA graduate who was a member of a wealthy L.A. furniture-store family, Barker Bros., urged me to go there. But the great Gardnar Mulloy offered me a scholarship to Miami – he was an undergraduate, but he ran the program for the university -- and that's where I went, enrolling in the fall of 1937.

I chose Miami instead of returning to L.A. to attend

---

* Toto moved to L.A. during World War II and was selling Lacoste shirts and teaching. I don't know how a Frenchman got interested in football, but every year for a while he and Southern California tennis honcho Perry Jones would go together to the Rose Bowl game. I accompanied them a number of times. Toto became a wonderful friend of mine. Years later, when my wife and I toured Europe, he showed us all the sights in Paris

UCLA or USC mainly because I wanted to play on clay. I was such a net-rusher that my ground strokes were terrible and I knew clay would be great training for ground strokes. Another thing, they had a wonderful winter circuit down there. All the hotels and country clubs had tennis tournaments one week after another, and the top players in the States would be there.

Our ``campus'' was an old hotel converted into a university. In the suburb of Coral Gables, where it is now, they were building a beautiful campus when the Depression came and they had to stop. They didn't have the money to finish. With the money they did have, they bought this old hotel and installed classrooms. We didn't have any tennis courts, so the Miami Biltmore turned its courts over to us to play and practice on.

Mulloy had started there in about 1931, when there was no tennis team. When he was a sophomore, he went to the president, Dr. B.F. Ashe, and convinced him to start a team with Gardnar in charge and on a tennis scholarship. The Hurricanes won the intercollegiate title in 1936, beating Harvard, Cornell, Princeton, Pennsylvania and Georgia on the way.

You couldn't play varsity as a freshman in those days, but I played in all those tournaments. The first thing of note, Mulloy, who was a senior, and I won the Miami Biltmore doubles, beating Bobby Riggs and Wayne Sabin in the semis. I had three good wins over first-10 players, Charlie Harris, a tough clay-courter, and Sabin at a tournament in Sarasota.

Mulloy and I became close friends, and I was best man at his big wedding. Actually they were already married, but her father didn't know that. He was a doctor and wanted this huge party. Bobby Riggs was there, Jack Kramer was there. I remember Riggs wanted to try on his tux, so he had me hold this big wad of bills he carried with him.

Mulloy was a great guy, helpful in any way he could, on or off the court. Then and for a long time afterward, he was also a great player. Not only has he won five major doubles titles (one Wimbledon and four U.S.) and 60 or so age-group titles over 30 or 40 years, but he is one of the greatest all-around athletes who ever played tennis.

He weighed about 160 pounds and was about 6-2, so he wasn't exactly prime football material. But they wanted him out for the team because he could kick and throw the ball farther than anybody on the varsity. At the end of the year, the university had what it called Field Day, where it had all-sports competition among the fraternities and other organizations on campus. And Gar won the diving. And he won an event in the swimming. And he was on the school boxing team.*

---

\* Along with all this, he was an intense, determined competitor. I'll jump ahead a lot of years to illustrate that. Former University of Georgia men's tennis coach Dan Magill, in his book ``Match Pointers,'' tells of an exhibition doubles match in Athens, Ga. Dennis Ralston, former USC star and former SMU coach, was teamed with country singer Kenny Rogers vs. baseball immortal Hank Aaron and Gardnar.

On their match point,'' wrote Magill, ``Dennis — as prearranged — hit an easy serve to Hank, who smacked the ball higher than any tennis ball I have ever seen hit. Swinging with two hands, exactly like he hit a baseball, he sent it soaring high over the Hall of Fame building, and as he hit the ball, the stadium P.A. announcer, whom I had alerted, said, `Number 756 – a new record for Hammerin' Hank Aaron!' The big crowd cheered loudly; but guess what an incensed Gardnar Mulloy did? He demanded that the point be replayed.''

Gar and I played in Birmingham, Alabama, the summer after my freshman year – the Cotton States Championship. Mulloy lost to a fellow in the semis, and I played that fellow in the

At West Palm Beach, they had a tournament. Charlie Harris was in the final with Mulloy. The night before, they went out to a carnival where they had this sledge hammer/gong contest. Gar could hit the gong every time; he had the timing. He would step aside and wait until a real, big husky guy came along who couldn't ring the gong. And no sooner had the husky guy put the sledge hammer down but Gar would step up, grab it and BONG, BONG. He had fun showing up the husky guys.

He lost in the final the next day 0, 0 and 0.

Bobby Riggs went to Miami the year before I went there, but he didn't stay. Mulloy had to wake him up every morning; he couldn't get him to go to class. Bobby wasn't interested, so he dropped out.

Riggs visited us at Miami my frosh year. He was driving a Cord, the most famous custom car in Hollywood, I think one of the first with front-wheel drive.

I had fairly good results my second summer on the circuit, in 1938. At Seabright, N.J., in August, according to American Lawn Tennis, ``Two results that may have surprised some were the win of Gardnar Mulloy and George Toley over (Gregory) Mangin and Gill Hall. … but in both cases the winning couples are well established and have other scalps hanging to their

---

final and beat him fairly easily. After the match, Mulloy said, ``You certainly wouldn't have won if you'd had to play me.''

When Mulloy was inducted into the Collegiate Tennis Hall of Fame at Athens, Magill kidded him about his claim to have been Pancho Segura's coach at Miami when the Ecuadorian won the NCAA singles title three straight years during World War II. Magill asked Mulloy how he could have commanded a landing craft in the Italy and Normandy invasions and coached Pancho at the same time. Mulloy replied, ``By postcards.''

belts." Also: ``Toley showed singles ability in downing Hall in two long sets."

I lost to Mulloy in the second round at Longwood and to Joe Hunt in the third round at Rye. But I surprised Don McNeill earlier at Rye -- ``Toley played smart tennis to earn a fine victory," said the reporter from American Lawn Tennis. Also in that magazine: ``The win of Toley and Gardnar Mulloy over Lewis Wetherell and Ronald Lubin, not unexpected except for the dispatch with which it was accomplished at 6-3, 6-4."

At the Longwood Cricket Club in Brookline, the grass courts were immaculate. I remember one year I arrived for the tournament and I walked out on the porch of the clubhouse and you couldn't see one dark spot on maybe 40 courts. Beautiful. They played like greased lightning. Mulloy and I got to the quarters of the National Doubles and we went to the referee of the tournament, Dwight Davis (of Davis Cup fame), and asked him if we could practice for just five minutes on the court, because the matches that day were over.

He acted as if we had just asked if we could screw his wife. That's the starchiest tennis club in the whole United States – Longwood Cricket Club. My friend Stan Drobac played there two or three years and never got to practice on grass. The only time he got to tread on it was for a match or if a member would invite him to play.

On we went to Southampton, Longwood again for the Invitation Bowl, Newport, and finally, in September, Forest Hills, where Don Budge beat my future fellow Trojan Gene Mako in the final. It was Don's second straight U.S. singles title. I got through the second round via default, then lost to McNeill 6-1, 6-4, 6-1.

After Forest Hills, Mark Buxby from Miami, said,

``George, the Naval Academy is opening up some tennis courts. Joe Hunt is a plebe there and they want to have some exhibitions to inaugurate the courts. Do you want to come along?" And I said, ``Sure."

(Joe Hunt was a handsome L.A. guy who was NCAA doubles champion at USC with Lewis Wetherell the previous season. He was to be NCAA singles champ for Navy in 1941 and U.S. singles champ at Forest Hills in 1943 while on leave from the Atlantic fleet. He died during a training flight in a Grumman Hellcat 19 miles off the coast of Daytona Beach, Fla., early in 1944. He was only 24, 15 days short of his 25th birthday.)

We spent four days at the Naval Academy and they treated us great. We stayed at a place called the Boat House, where we had TWO cooks. Every morning they asked us what we wanted for our meals. We played the exhibitions and then there was an exhibition arranged in Philadelphia. After those exhibitions, we went to a banquet at the Philadelphia Athletic Club. We walked out of the club at 11 o'clock at night and we were going to drive down to Miami the next morning to go back to school.

Practically right across the street was the YMCA and we decided to sleep there for about four hours before getting underway. As we walked into the lobby, the clerk put the phone down and as he was putting it down he said, ``He's not here." The only thing I heard was the T part; I didn't catch the rest of the name. We got to the desk and I said, ``Who was that call for?" He said, ``For a Toley." I said, ``That happens to be me."

My sisters had been trying to get hold of me for a week because my mother was ill. So that morning, instead of heading back to Miami with Buxby, I took a plane for L.A. My mother recovered from that illness, but

I decided to stay home. One of my doubles partners, Ronald Lubin, who later became a Hollywood producer, was at USC and he was the one who was responsible for talking me into transferring there.

``You're going to come in, but we don't have a full scholarship for you," he said. ``We'll give you a half-scholarship and then you'll have a job, which will take care of the other half."

Before classes in the morning I used to clean up rooms and stuff like that. Then the second semester, they didn't offer me the second half and I never asked them for it. I was No. 1 on the team and never had a full scholarship. They only had three or four in those days.

Anyway, I enrolled there in the fall of 1938, changing the course of my life.

## TOLEY'S TIPS - 2

*SIMULTANEOUSLY SLICE AND PUNCH*: Most volleys should be sliced – punched but sliced. Even some of the volleys you put away with power should be sliced – punch them, but slice them as you punch. The whole secret of the volley is to keep under the ball. You have better feel and you can drop volley. An opponent can hit the ball at you 90 miles an hour and you slice it right back to the baseline nice and slow.

I'm particularly a stickler for low volleys having underspin. It's the only way you can have consistent control of the shot. Use the flat volley under ideal conditions – when near the net and the ball is high enough to use a downward trajectory.

*LONG STEP ON THE FIRST VOLLEY*: This is for the net-rusher. Serve and run to the net as fast as you can. A right-hander's last step before punching that volley should be a long one. For a forehand volley, the left foot is forward. For a backhand volley, the right foot is forward. I want that forward foot to hit the ground as the ball is struck. Jack Kramer did this, always getting inside the service line for that first volley, his forward foot touching down as the ball was struck.

I told my students, ``Don't do anything with that first volley unless you have an absolute setup. Just get it back down to the opponent's feet. If he gets it back down to your feet, then back to his feet again.'' This is, of course, easier to do in doubles because you have less court to cover.

*LOSE THE SHUFFLE*: Some teachers advocate running in after serving, stopping and shuffling your feet, but all that does is impede your progress to the net. In fact, it makes it harder to get to balls because if the return is wide, you're losing a step or two in getting to the ball.

*DON'T BE SHY OF THAT NET*: In volleying, get as close to the net as you possibly can. You can meet the ball on your side and then reach over the net. By doing this you are improving your chances of putting the ball away, because you have a better angle and you're getting the ball back to your opponent quicker. Whenever you're hitting down, you can hit it harder.

# USC AND
# BACK TO THE CIRCUIT

Bob Lutz
(Photo courtesy of World Championship Tennis)

## USC AND
## BACK TO THE CIRCUIT

For the 1938-39 season, because I was a transfer, I just practiced with the team. Then in 1940, USC was the best in the nation by far. I played No. 1, Frederick "Ted" Schroeder, who was a sophomore, was 2, and we had Ken Bartlett, Marvin Carlock, Myron McNamara and William Reedy. We had tennis players there – oh, it was unbelievable.

Our coach, Harold Godshall, wrote this in a letter to *American Lawn Tennis*: "George is a transfer from the University of Miami, where he went after a thorough tennis schooling in Los Angeles. He traveled extensively last summer and was seen in all national tournaments. He is a junior and is expected to be the most consistent man on the team."

Godshall, busy with his insurance business, didn't do any actual coaching. He never came to practices. The players figured out the lineup. Tennis was not high on the athletic department's priority list.

A funny thing happened between Schroeder and me. We were at the national doubles and I was walking to the locker room and he was going to the courts. He had just won the national junior singles, so I congratulated him. And he pulled a faux pas, which was typical. He said, "You and Ronnie Lubin will be a good second doubles team next year."

I made up my mind that I was going to beat him and play No. 1, and I won the first challenge match. In the second challenge match, I think I won in straight sets. He broke his racket on the net post and cried!

One summer about this time, we were in Boston for the national doubles – Schroeder and Jack Kramer were defending champions. Kramer wanted to go to Spalding headquarters for some rackets – this was before his long affiliation with Wilson. Bitsy Grant lent him his car and I went along, because I was also on the Spalding free list. On the way back we saw Schroeder standing in front of the Wilson headquarters and gave him a ride.

Kramer had a program on the radio. Schroeder reached through from the back seat and changed the station. Kramer politely let it go for a block or two, then changed it back to his program. Schroeder right away changed it again. Now Jack was pissed off.

"God damn it, Schroeder," he said, "this is Bitsy Grant's car, I borrowed it, I'm in charge of it, I'm going to listen to my program."

Schroeder yelled out, "Stop the car." He got out of the car, reached back into the back seat, picked up a handful of our rackets, slammed them down on the floor and stalked off.

That's the kind of guy he was.

Kramer somehow managed to stay friendly with Ted through the years. I can't say the same for me. Schroeder transferred to Stanford after that season and most of us were not sorry to see him go.

But I must give Ted Schroeder credit. He was a hell of a competitor – the best competitor, I would say

– even better than Bobby Riggs. Bobby was a terrific competitor, but Schroeder was something above. He was a net-rusher and a good volleyer. Medium size and moved well. I played him in the national clay courts singles and I won the first set and had him 5-1 in the second. He won that second set and the match. When he got down, he would start hitting out, and he would make them. That's what he did once when in three matches he had nine match points against him at Wimbledon.

"Lucky Ted" Schroeder, as some British sportswriters called him, won Wimbledon singles in 1949 and became the first champion to receive his trophy on the court. He survived four five-set matches that year – against Gardnar Mulloy of the U.S., Frank Sedgman of Australia, Eric Sturgess of South Africa and, in the final, Jaroslav Drobny of Czechoslovakia -- which I say is more courageous than lucky.

In April of my first year on the Trojan team, we smashed UCLA 8-1. In the longest match of the afternoon, I beat the Bruins' Bob Stanford 6-2, 3-6, 9-7. We won the rematch with UCLA, but Stanford beat me in another three-setter, 6-1, 2-6, 6-0. J.D. Morgan, who later became famous as a fine athletic director at UCLA, was on its tennis squad that year.

Wrote Frank Stewart in American Lawn Tennis, "University of Southern California's superbly balanced varsity of Ted Schroeder, George Toley, Bill Reedy, Myron McNamara, captain Ken Bartlett and Leon Everett captured every team and individual honor in Pacific Coast Competition this year."

But at the 56th national collegiates, I lost in the fourth round to Billy Talbert of Cincinnati, on clay. Schroeder and I lost in the semis of doubles to guys we had beaten at the Ojai, California, tournament 2 and 2. And Schroeder was eliminated by Talbert. Don McNeill of Kenyon was NCAA champion that year; he beat Joe Hunt of Navy in the final. Schroeder was to win in 1942 for Stanford, just before Pancho Segura started his string of three straight singles titles for Miami.

At the Eastern Intercollegiates at Montclair, N.J., in early July, I beat George Parks of Miami, Henry Batjer of Texas, Bobby Low of Stanford, Charles Rider of North Carolina and Joe Fishbach of St. John's – a long haul on hard clay. Then I beat teammate McNamara in the semis and Northwestern's Seymour Greenberg in the final, 6-3, 6-2, 6-4. "Toley had it all over Greenberg," said the Associated Press, "as he displayed his best form of the tournament." The *American Lawn Tennis* correspondent complimented my "judicious acceptance" of the opportunities Greenberg presented me. We won the team title over Stanford, 40 points to 18.

The rest of the summer went fairly well. A one-sided, straight-set loss to Jack Kramer at Baltimore in the fourth round. Lost in the second round at Rye, N.Y., to H.J. Prusoff in three sets. Reached the third round at Newport Casino and lost there to Don McNeill. A big win was in late August on clay over Bryan "Bitsy" Grant of Atlanta at the Seigniory Club in Canada. This is from *American Lawn Tennis*:

"Toley was an inspired player against Grant. His speedy drives were working to perfection and his long legs covered every inch of the court, even though he started out with a deficit of five games."

The funny thing about it, Bitsy and I were practicing on grass before we went up there, and he kept beating me on grass. He was considered one of the top two or three players in the world on clay for 10 years. I remember he was beating me, leading me 4-1 and I was tight and nervous, and all of a sudden I said to myself, "God all mighty, you know he's going to win. He's beaten you. Just relax and have some fun." And all of a sudden, I beat him in straight sets.

That year,1940,  I missed making the top 10 in America by one point.

I was playing Frank Kovacs at the quarters at Southampton. He was from San Francisco and was one of the top three in the world. I had seven match points in the second set. Once, I had 40-love on my serve, and another time I had 40-15 on my serve to win the match. Out of those seven match points, I made only one error. He would just knock off a winner every time. The first one, he just ran in and hit the ball before coming in to shake hands with me, because I was serving at 5-1 and 40-0. He just slammed the ball and the chalk flew in the air. Finally, at about 12-all, he was serving and I had match point, and I decided to go for it. I missed by about a foot. Final score: 4-6, 14-12, 6-1. The next day Kovacs went out and beat Bobby Riggs.

A win that day would have put me in the first 10.

It was not the only time I blew a lead. I lost a marathon match to Earl Cochell at the L.A. Tennis Club that same year. I led 5-1 in the third set and lost 6-8, 6-3, 12-10.

## TOLEY'S TIPS - 3

*NOT BLOWING A LEAD:* Sometimes, an opponent who is down and almost out will relax, start hitting with abandon – or just raise his or her game -- and make a comeback. Some players have success at holding a big lead by stepping up the pressure, playing or hitting harder. A few have success by becoming steadier or more conservative. Usually, you should stick with what got you there.

*GO WITH THE WIND:* When the wind is at your back, go to the net, because it slows down your opponent's shots and adds velocity to your own. And cut down on the velocity of your serve in order to keep it in the court.

If there is a swirling wind, you're in trouble, but so is your opponent. My friend Stan Drobac says it is "the greatest equalizer in the world." The worst NCAA Tournament we ever played in was in Corpus Christi, Texas – 30-mile-an-hour winds, day and night. The players were nervous wrecks. In those conditions, I had my players let lobs bounce. And if the wind was blowing across the court to the opponent's right, use a slice serve, which will be accentuated.

# SENIOR YEAR AND EARLY
# DAYS AS A PRO

Dennis Ralston
(Photo courtesy of the USC Sports Archives)

## SENIOR YEAR AND
## EARLY DAYS AS A PRO

I was a married man before I was a college graduate. Back when I was 17, I was working in a pro shop across the street from Echo Park in Los Angeles — stringing rackets mostly — and playing tennis on the park courts. There I met a 15-year-old tennis player named Miriam Grady, but I thought she was my age. She lived fairly near the courts and I asked her out. So the first date I went to pick her up and her mother said, "Now, George, she's got to be home by at least 11."

She was really my first and only girlfriend. We had dated for four years and the war was coming on, so we decided to get married. I gave up playing tennis that fall semester and then in the spring semester I just played in the team matches.

I had been ushering at USC football and ice hockey games and had saved about $300, which in those days was like $3,000 now. I took a final exam, and in those days we could drive a car right up to outside the classroom. I came out from the final and Miriam and I took off for three months and one week – traveled the tennis circuit and had a great time.

After our honeymoon, we came home and the next day my USC teammate Ron Lubin called me and said there was an opening at the Beverly Hills Tennis Club. The people at the club wanted me to stay out of USC for a semester and work there, then work there the next semester while finishing school. I was the pro there for two and a half months and the manager left, so I took that job, too.

Before my last semester started, men's tennis coach Godshall was killed in a car accident. Athletic Director Willis O. Hunter called and asked if I would be coach of the team. I said, "Sure." So that last semester I was married, taking 11 units, managing and coaching at the club and coaching the USC team.

My Trojans, with me, Charles "Ted" Olewine, Bill Reedy, Charles Mattman, Ronald Lubin and Marvin Carlock, were undefeated in league play in 1940-41. Olewine, whom I didn't even challenge to see who would play No. 1, won the singles at Ojai. Reedy and Mattman won doubles.

At the intercollegiates, Olewine lost in the final to Hunt of Navy, but he and Mattmann won the doubles.

Ted Olewine was a wonderful person, jovial. Everybody liked him. He was one of many good players who have come out of Santa Monica and he won a lot of matches against Jack Kramer. He didn't have a lot of power, but he was a good competitor. Ted almost flunked out of USC his first semester — he got too involved in fraternity life — but he never had any academic trouble after that. Like Joe Hunt, he died young. He caught some disease in the service in the war and died soon after.

Bill Tilden, who was from Pennsylvania but had moved out to California in that era, was the greatest at intimidating officials. He was a son of a bitch who did everything he could get away with in a match. Pancho Gonzalez was the same way.

Santa Ana High School down in Orange County had some new courts, so to inaugurate them, there was an exhibition. The kids paid 25 cents to watch. Tilden and Les Stoefen first played singles, then John Faunce and I played Tilden and Stoefen in doubles. John and I won the first set and we had a break in the second set. A disputed point came up, although the ball was definitely called right.

Tilden wouldn't play for five minutes. He was fuming and storming around in front of the young kids. What was at stake, other than his innate desire to win, was before the match we agreed that whoever won the doubles would get the gate. I think it was his strong desire to win, more than the money angle.

And he was a crook. He and this other guy at the Beverly Hills Tennis Club wouldn't pay up when they lost at cards, but they'd collect when they won. So the members finally got fed up and they complained to the management, so we had to tell Bill Tilden he was no longer welcome at the club.

He wasn't a very nice person. In those later years, he was sloppy in his dress. He was noted for being a terrible coach and most people he worked with didn't ever amount to a damn. He taught one kid who was pretty good in the 15-year-old division, and that was it.

But he certainly was a great talent, one of the greatest players who ever walked on a court. I saw him play Ellsworth Vines at the Olympic Auditorium in L.A.

Indoors was ideal for Elly's game but not for Tilden's. Tilden was 39 years old, and yet it took Vines four hours to beat him in five long sets.

My fifth and last summer on the eastern circuit — that was 1941 — I had one of my best wins, in Ocean City, Md., at the Atlantic Coast Championships. I beat the great Gene Mako in the semifinals 7-5, 6-4. Said *American Lawn Tennis*:

"In the semi-final round Mako met his Nemesis, otherwise George Toley. ... Mako was decidedly not on and Toley had slipped a little. Consequently the match was close and good shots and errors were much in evidence. A victory in straight sets put Toley in striking distance of winning the event.

"It is not often that one sees such a ding-dong match as the one between (Ted) Olewine and Toley in the final round match. Five sets were required for Olewine to secure the victory; all of them except the fifth were won at 6-1; and Toley led at two sets to one, and even in the final set looked as if he might well triumph. There was a great deal of variation in Toley's game. He was very good at times and his drives, volleys, serves and smashes were fine to watch; he sent over three service aces in succession at one time. But mixed in ... were many errors, some of them apparently quite inexcusable. Olewine was the work horse. He stayed back most of the time, diving doggedly and with excellent judgment. He made mistakes but they were not as numerous and disastrous as those of Toley. In the fifth set both men were feeling the strain and yet they fought as fiercely as at the beginning of the match . ... The set went to Olewine finally and to the very end it was a miracle of closeness; two or three shots resulting differently would have changed the result."

My spirits were lifted a lot by winning the doubles with William Gillespie over Mako and Olewine 7-9, 7-5, 6-3.* And I won the mixed doubles with Millicent Hurst Lang.

I couldn't repeat as Eastern Intercollegiates champ. Greenberg won it this time after I lost in the semis to Ronald Edwards of San Jose State in four sets. At Forest Hills in September (won by Riggs), I fell to Don McNeill in the second round in straight sets. But after the East Jersey Challenge Bowl, I at least got another good notice from American Lawn Tennis:

"The meeting of Toley and (Eddie) Moylan was perhaps the best of the tournament. George, serving beautifully, took the first set at 11-9 but Moylan's passing shots were too much for him the second and he lost it at 7-5. Moylan hit well off both forehand and backhand and seemed to pass Toley at will. However, Toley made a game bid in the third and Moylan had to play superlative tennis to win."

The 1941 national rankings had Riggs and Kovacs at Nos. 1 and 2, Greenberg and me at 19 and 20.

---

* Gene Mako, born in Hungary but reared in Glendale, California, was a tremendous talent. He hardly ever lost a set in the junior divisions and was a terrific player at USC 1934-36. He was the Trojans' first NCAA singles champ, in 1934, and the same year he and Phillip Caslin were the school's first NCAA doubles champs.

A shoulder injury hampered his serve somewhere along the way, but he still was an important doubles partner with the great Don Budge. I saw his last match in the national doubles, he and Budge versus Australia's John Bromwich and Adrian Quist, a great team. Bromwich was the greatest deuce-court player, winning 13 Grand Slam doubles with three different partners. That day, I thought Mako was the best man on the court, because he hit drop shots and lob volleys and did everything like a magician, as if he had a magic wand. It was his last match with Budge.

## TOLEY'S TIPS - 4

*THE EYES HAVE IT:* Don Budge had fantastic eyes, plus he had fast reflexes. In all the time I watched him play or played against him – and we played a lot because after World War II he spent a lot time at the L.A. Tennis Club – the guy was never caught off guard. Never! He was always there waiting for the ball. It's the eyes. Despite the heavy racket he used (17 ounces), in a fast doubles exchange at the net he was never late. You never caught him being awkward. Seeing that ball so early, he was always ready.

Eyes are more important in tennis than most people think. Why are some people stronger with the forehand than the backhand or vice versa? The left eye for a right-hander is important for the forehand. On the backhand side it's the right eye. Some people can actually focus better off one side than the other. It might be a good idea for coaches to check players for which eye is dominant, and develop the weaker side.

Chuck Carr won our Southern Cal men's title one year. His eyes were so sharp that when he hit that ball he hit in the middle of that racket absolutely every time. His sound was always the same, always perfect.

# THE MECCA

Rafael Osuna
(Photo courtesy of Rafael Belmar Osuna)

# THE MECCA

The Los Angeles Tennis Club, so important in my personal history and in the history of tennis, began in 1920 during the presidency of Warren Harding. Captain A.C.B. Gray, manager of the club, wrote in the 1930 program for the Pacific Southwest tournament, "When Vine Street down from Hollywood Boulevard was a little more than a passable roadway lined with pepper trees, and Melrose was an unpaved `cowpath' with street cars and buses unthought of, the Los Angeles Tennis Club was born on the spot where it now stands."

It stands there today, tucked away on Clinton Street, just north of the Wilshire Country Club and just southwest of Paramount Studios and the Hollywood Forever Cemetery.

Before I landed my job there, I and hundreds of thousands of others had World War II to worry about. After Pearl Harbor, I tried to get into the Naval Air Corps as a pilot and was turned down. Then I considered joining the Navy as a gunnery officer. Eventually I served in the Army Air Corps as a physical trainer. I was a master sergeant at first, then went to officer-candidate school in Miami, emerging as a second lieutenant. Most of my duty was performed in Texas, and Miriam could live with me. Among other things, I ran an aquatics-safety program, taught parachuting airmen how to tumble when they hit the ground and how to deflate the chute so they wouldn't be dragged.

During the war, I played no tennis. We were so busy that I never noticed if there were courts at the places I was stationed.

After the war, I was going to go into the cement-block-making business with my wife's uncle. I wasn't thinking seriously about tennis. It wasn't on my mind at all. Then one day I was walking past a tennis-teaching school on La Cienega one block below Wilshire. The owner, a fellow named Craig, came running out of the shop and said, "George, you're just the guy that's going to run my business." Like that! The contract was too good to turn down, a $500-a-month guarantee. I was there over a year.

I also taught at some private courts, and some of my kids were students at Marlborough School, a prestigious private school for girls. One day I was driving one of the girls home and a couple of other girls came up to the car and said, "Oh, Mr. Toley, we hear you're going to be the professional at Marlborough." I didn't know anything about it. But I was offered the job within a week, and at about the same time, the pro at the L.A. Tennis Club left. The club was just a few blocks from the school, so I took both jobs. The year was 1946.

Marlborough had more than a little tennis history, most of it in the person of Elizabeth "Bunny" Ryan, who went there in the early 1900s and won interscholastic and Ojai Tournament championships. She became Suzanne Lenglen's doubles partner and the winner of 19 Wimbledon titles – 12 women's doubles and seven mixed doubles. She also won the U.S. doubles in 1926 and the French doubles four times in the 1930s.

She was a delightful gal, very enthusiastic. I gave her a tennis lesson when she was 80 or so. She was around the club often. She died of a heart attack in 1979 in England (where she lived most of her life) less than 24 hours before Billie Jean King surpassed her record by winning a 20th title.

We had national champions while I was at Marlborough. Nancy Dwyer won the national girls' 18 doubles in 1953, for instance. Hillary Hilton and Kris Kemmer were multiple national winners.

The rules for Marlborough girls were very strict. They couldn't chew gum. When we went to Ojai for the big annual tournament, if they chewed gum, we sent them home. The girls had to have their blouses tucked in at all times. There was a Marlborough teacher who had her eyes peeled all the time in that area, where the girls were exercising. She'd yell all across the yard, "Alice, you get that shirt in!" That's the way it was.

*Mel Calvin* (The former Mary Eleanor Lafever): George was just wonderful. I think we all had a crush on him. He was so handsome – those dark glasses.

I remember we would play matches at the tennis club, getting ready to see who would be on the team. We'd go and try to get on the farthest court away so nobody could see us. We were having a match one day and having rallies that went on forever and ever. My opponent would call one out and I knew it wasn't out, and then I'd call one out and it really wasn't. It was just terrible. All of a sudden, I heard his voice. He said, "Mel, I think you and Valerie should stop now and you can finish this match another day."

Down below that court was where George did all his work on the rackets and he had been watching us. It was so embarrassing. But he was so kind. He never said anything but "Play it over again tomorrow."

However, probably the best girl I ever coached was not a student at Marlborough and not a member of the club. She was Sally Moore, whose dad would drive her down from Bakersfield in the San Joaquin Valley to take lessons starting at about age 11. She won the national girls' 18 singles in 1956 and 1957, won junior Wimbledon and rose to No. 4 among U.S. women in 1959. As a married woman and mother in the 1980s, she won a number of age-group tournaments – singles and doubles — on hard courts and clay.

I was pleased with my work on Sally's backhand. I taught that stroke like the Japanese use judo to break a board, focusing on the elbow and the wrist. I had them just straighten out their arm and point. Didn't even follow through at the beginning. I wouldn't let a student use her shoulder, just the arm and elbow. No jarring involved at all. Just straighten it out. Usually I had them do that for a length of time, then I'd add the follow-through. But Sally's backhand was terrific, especially down the line – she could hit the hell out of the ball. I left it alone.

> *Sally Moore*: My father drove me down every weekend for lessons. Sometimes my father would drive me back that night and drive me back down the next day for another lesson. Sometimes George would arrange for me to play somebody there at the club. Or work on the ball machines. It took an interested parent, because in those days there were no clinics and no tennis academies.
>
> It was determined when I was young, when I started, that I would be champion of the world — by the two of us, my dad and me. That was the goal. It wasn't to be a player, it was never to be a player. It was to be champion. If you won Wimbledon, you were champion of the world. That was it.

I won the juniors at Wimbledon when I was 18. At 19 I was a semifinalist there. But I kept losing my forehand. In the old days, you would have these grooved strokes and you would lose them. ... I got on some fast grass and my rhythm got off and I lost the forehand. I was talking to George over the phone. He said, "Go get a coach, get him to do this. Hit the ball to out here, throw the balls to you like this." All this tennis stuff he was trying to get me through. Oh, it was terrible.

George almost came over. I think he would have flown over if I had gotten to the finals. Then I flew right back to L.A. to work with George, because I had no forehand. He started like he always did, dropping balls, regrooving – right from kindergarten. ... It was so painful, this process was so awful, I can tell you.

George was a master. He was great, wonderful. He was very professional – not distant, just very, very professional. He was like a second father to me. Very exact in what he wanted, very precise. Then he'd grab my hand and take me through the motion, to make sure I had it right.

I remember one match when Sally was in the 15s. There was a girl from San Diego who was beating her. And this girl had a terrific forehand. So I watched her play and she would back up to hit forehands way in the backhand court. When she did this, she could keep that forehand in a groove, gain confidence and rally Sally off the court.

So I said, "Sally, I don't want you to hit two balls in a row to her backhand. I want you to go down the line and *then* you hit it crosscourt, so she has to hit her backhand." So now the other girl wasn't hitting forehand after forehand, wasn't getting into that groove. It made a tremendous difference in the match.

She is Sally Moore Huss now, with a beautiful home in La Jolla, a thriving art/decoration business — wallpaper and bedspreads and all sorts of attractive goods. And she has her own Web site (www.Sallyhuss.com). She's written and illustrated at least two tennis books, *How to Play Power Tennis* and *Sneakers, A Courtside Book of Tennis Humor*.

Sally got along great with my wife, who had a little art studio at our house. Sally's first easel was a gift from Miriam.

Maybe the best teen-age boy I ever coached, tall, skinny Howard Schoenfield, didn't work out so well. A doctor's son, he was born in Texas but grew up in Minnesota and started to play tennis at age 8. When he was 13, the family moved to Beverly Hills. In the mid-1970s he won nine national titles in the 16s and 18s, and I was quoted in the L.A. Times on him in November of '73: "Tennis means everything to him. He practices long hours and will stick to a practice schedule. He will do whatever I tell him until he drops."

Personal problems derailed Howard's career and he never became the college star he should have been, much less an adult player of international stature.

The restaurant contributed to the warm, friendly atmosphere of the L.A. Tennis Club. For years and years, we had a cook, Maude, who made the greatest pies. I would arrive at the club after a morning session at Marlborough, have my lunch and follow it with two pies a la mode. She always saved them for me. The pies went fast.

*Sashi Menon* (USC letterman 1971-72-73-74): I was hardly off the plane from India and George took me for my first day at the L.A. Tennis Club. He showed me around, then took me into the restaurant for lunch. There was a waitress there, Dee, who didn't have a lot of patience.

She said, "What do you want?"

George had to get up and take a phone call, but before he left he said, "You've got to try the hamburger."

I said, "I'll have a hamburger."

"How do you want it done?" she asked.

I had no idea what she was talking about. I'd been to Europe, but I had never had a hamburger. I didn't say anything.

She stared and me and asked, "What do you want on it?"

Now I was really stumped. Finally I said, "Everything."

So that was the first hamburger for a Hindu boy from Puna, outside of Bombay. When George came back and I told him about it, he was laughing.

Menon adjusted to America quickly. He lettered four years at USC, 1971-74, was a three-time All-America, played on the pro circuit and settled into a beautiful home in San Juan Capistrano, with a successful career as a financial adviser. Even though he was a Davis Cup stalwart for India for some years, he became Americanized.

He is *very* married, by the way, to an Indian woman from Goa he met in Australia. They were wed in Pittsburgh in a civil ceremony, then had a Hindu wedding to please his parents, then a Catholic wedding to please her parents. India has many languages and the Menons don't speak each other's, so they and their children converse in English.

Our only child, Katie, was born in 1955, not long after I took the job, so many of her earliest, and I think happiest, memories have to do with the club. (She's now Katie Dempster, a USC graduate, attorney and mother of two sons.)

*Katie Dempster*: When I was probably 6 or 7, I became aware of the sport of tennis … I wanted my father to teach me, but he refused, insisting I was too young. Now, of course, people start even younger, but back then he refused to teach me or even put me on a tennis court with a racket and a ball until I was 9 years old.

So at 9, probably around my birthday, we got out on a tennis court and I hit my first forehand, learned how to actually hit a ball over the net. I remember we were at the Los Angeles Tennis Club, on one of the back courts, probably his old teaching court, No. 12. It was just the two of us and for many days and many years it would be just the two of us on that back court, hitting balls against a ball machine or dropping balls and hitting them.

Dad spent most of his time on that tennis court. He would teach from the early hours in the morning until the late hours in the afternoon, as long as there was daylight – so longer in the summertime.

I grew up mostly waiting for him at the club. When I was in elementary school, I would go on the weekends and play some tennis and learn from him, and then basically wait around for him to be finished so we could go home. I remember that I liked to work in the tennis shop, which he operated for the club. My mother would keep the books and do the billing and accounts payable and receivable, and charge the members for lessons and things like that.

It was a very small tennis shop located under the center-court bleachers. I remember I loved to organize and clean up the shop, and he got the biggest kick out of that. I think I have my father's organization gene, because he was in officer-candidate school in the big war, World War II, and developed extremely organized and clean habits. My father is meticulous.

Teaching gave me much more income than the shop, which was kind of a hassle. But the board of directors expected the pro to run the shop as part of the job. They got a percentage of my gross. I had a wonderful bookkeeper. My wife Miriam did all the books for me.

Balls were always the biggest profit, rackets and stringing second. Usually, after matches, players would stop by the store and say, "So and so will pay for the balls. They lost." And we'd put the losers' names on the ticket, or bill, for the balls. At the end of the day, I would take those tickets home to Miriam. Our prices were competitive. In fact, I had an understanding with the board that my ball prices would be commensurate with other places in town. I would call other tennis shops and find out what their prices were.

We carried Spalding, Dunlop and Wilson. Maybe Slazenger, too. But in all the years I was there, 97 percent of the balls used were Wilson. The company took great care with their tennis balls. For instance, I could go to Joe Bixler, the Wilson representative, and say, "Joe, those balls haven't been lasting very long," and right away Joe would get out there and test them and call back to the factory for an adjustment.

Wilson and I had a wonderful setup because of Bixler. My SC guys all used Wilson equipment. They could walk into my shop and get a racket or anything they wanted. They would take the sales slip and put it in the Wilson box and Joe would take care of it.

Right after the war, practically all the top players in the world were at the club, because they were starting to get back into tennis.

Don Budge, who had won the Grand Slam eight years before, had a service problem in 1946. He just pushed it in, couldn't do anything with it. He had already started a professional tour with Bobby Riggs, and Riggs had won the first part of the tour simply because Don couldn't serve well. His overhead was affected, too.

One day he walked into the locker room and sat by the place where they dried their clothes. I was by my locker. He was dejected about his serve, and I had been wanting to say something to him about it. But I just felt I didn't have the right to say anything to the great Don Budge. Then it got so that I just couldn't hold it in.

I grabbed my teaching basket of balls and walked out of the locker room quickly, saying on my way out, "Don, if you get your elbow up where it belongs on your service motion, that will take care of it." That was all there was to it.

The next day he left with Riggs for the South African part of their tour. The day after they got back, he met me in the locker room and said, "George, I want you to help me with my serve. I saw some pictures of my serve before my (shoulder) injury and saw it was different. You're the only one who has mentioned that."

What had happened, because of the injury, when he

brought his arm down on the service motion and started up, his elbow would end up almost beside his body. To be right, the upper part of your arm should be parallel to the ground. No one had told him he was serving like a cripple almost.

We went to work and the first thing that happened, he wanted to serve right away. I said, "No, you're going to have to go through these exercises I'm going to give you and it's going to be maybe a month before you serve." He looked at me as if I was out of my noggin.

The first time he did the motion the right way, his face grimaced. "That's OK," he said. "I've talked to the doctor. He told me that I can stretch the scar tissue and I can get it back to where it used to be." So all I did, I would be alongside him and I would tell him how high the elbow was. I'd say, "Below level." Or "Parallel to the ground." He was great about it, and I know it hurt him. And he did exactly as I told him, without the racket, and eventually I put the racket in his hand, and he gradually got his arm to where should be. It took a couple of months almost. His serve just blossomed.

Later, the day after he got back from losing in a pro-tournament final at Forest Hills, he walked into the club and gave me a gold watch, engraved.

The big redhead had some good years left. He reached the U.S. Pro finals in 1946, 1947, 1949 and 1953. And on that 1946 tour, Riggs ended up barely besting him 23-21.

A huge presence at the club and in all of tennis was Perry Thomas Jones, head of the Southern California Tennis Association (SCTA) and future inductee into the International Tennis Hall of Fame. The SCTA is now headquartered at UCLA, but back then it was at the club – in two rooms.

He had been a good player, winning the L.A. city men's title in 1918. He began with the SCTA in the early 1920s, first as head of junior development, then in 1929 as secretary, then 1954 as president. He also published and edited a magazine, *Western Tennis*, 1936-1945.

"Many people thought he was wealthy," wrote Patricia Henry Yeomans in her book *Southern California Tennis Champions 1887-1987*. "He always dressed well, ate at the best places and visited famous resorts. The truth is, he lost his job at a savings & loan in Hollywood and had been working in a lumber yard to make ends meet." Then he became manager of the Pacific Southwest tournament and ran – I should say dominated – the SCTA."

There was a big problem between Jones and the club, and it was that it was like a gambling den there. Gin rummy and poker and backgammon where the dining room is now, so the juniors would have to walk back and forth through this atmosphere. Jones would tell parents not to have their children become members.

When I got the job, we had six active juniors, which made me unhappy. Then I got the job of coaching the girls from nearby Marlborough School and I made arrangements to have them get summer memberships, so they could play tennis and swim. When the girls came, that started some of the boys coming. The junior program started to build. Then we changed the architecture and made a card room off to the side, out of the way.

Jones supported the junior program with enthusiasm and a strict hand. When there was a good prospect in L.A. in the juniors, he wanted him at the club. The club always gave whatever Jones asked and I would help in deciding what the player's potential was. But he was certainly a tyrant. Things had to be done his way – and to be fair, his way was often a good way.

"Mark Winters wanted to go east and play in the U.S. Nationals at Kalamazoo," wrote Pat Yeomans in her book. "He knew the traditions. He got a haircut. He arrived at the SCTA office and presented himself and his itinerary to Mr. Jones, who smiled and patted him on the head, saying, `You've just had a haircut, haven't you?' Later his application was endorsed by SCTA but he was embarrassed to note SCTA refused to endorse several players ranked above him. They probably had shaggy hair."

Yeomans quoted Ellsworth Vines on Jones: "I really loved the old boy, even if he was obstinate and opinionated as to his dislikes either on the courts or to various players. However, I felt he was very fair."

*Jim Buck* (USC letterman 1957-58): Perry knew exactly what he wanted. I remember one time, Ed Atkinson was going back east and Jones said, "You're not going until you get a haircut." Gave him money for a haircut, which he went and got. Maria Bueno (a star player from Brazil) wouldn't wear a skirt to play the Pacific Southwest tournament and he wouldn't let her play on the first five courts unless she put on a skirt. She played on the backcourts.

He took a liking to me one year when I was going to play a northern circuit with my teammate Chuck Rombeau. There used to a circuit – Tacoma, Seattle, Portland, Vancouver, Victoria, and the last two were on grass. I was working that first week after school to get some money, working on a top of a building down in Vernon, using a crowbar to take the roof off. I blistered my hand pretty badly and

Jones said, "We can't have you doing that. You've got to keep your hands so you can play tennis!"

I said, "If I don't work, I don't go up north."

He said, "All right, I'll give you a job. I'll give you $75 a week and you be the roving foot-fault judge."

I said, "I can't do that. I'm making more at the other place."

He said, "I'll match it."

So I quit the roofing job and became a foot-fault judge to earn the money to go up there.

*Dick Leach* (USC letterman 1959-60-61, Toley's successor as USC men's coach): One time I was playing a match on the center court and my shoes had a little dirt on them, and he came out and said, "What size shoes do you wear?" I told him. He went into the pro shop, bought me a brand-new pair of shoes and came out and said, "Put these on." He wanted you to always have white shorts, white shirt, clean white shoes.

He told me that if you played in your warmup suit, you're being disrespectful of an opponent, and I believe that. It's true. Playing in a warmup suit, it's like you're saying the guy's no good and you don't even have to take off your sweats to beat him.

*Bill Bond* (USC letterman 1962-63-64): He was very opinionated. The funny thing is, you look at tennis today and rarely do you see a clean-shaven guy. Sometimes you see hair all over the place. And some players don't dress well. That wouldn't have happened with Perry Jones. I used to have a little cowlick in front and he didn't like that. He wanted me to have a short, butch haircut.

I'll never forget going into Perry's office. He was like the CEO of a big company or something. He had trophies all over. Very impressive. Unbelievable guy.

Along one wall, Jones had a big trophy case. He was quite a collector. He used to go to Europe and buy up trophies and he had a fabulous collection.

But it wasn't just pomp and circumstance in that little office. There was sweat produced – his playing days were over, but he gave his life over to tennis. I admired Perry. He worked very hard for long hours. I would go to the club late sometimes because I had some work to do in the shop – maybe 11 o'clock – and many times his light would be on.

*Alex Olmedo* (USC letterman 1956-57-58): When I came to this country from Peru – a boat from Peru to Cuba through the Panama Canal, a plane to Miami, a bus from Miami to L.A. — I played in the public parks – mostly at Poinsettia Park. I had a little difficulty with the language and the association, which was run by Perry T. Jones. About 1954-1955, I wanted to play in the Pacific Southwest juniors. I was 17. I went to the L.A. Tennis Club to see if I could get an entry blank. I was rejected on the grounds I wasn't going to school. I was going to night school to learn English at the time.

*Ed Atkinson* (USC letterman 1957-58-60): If he didn't like you, if you didn't do what he said, he could bar you from every tournament in the world.

He was tyrannical, he was racially bigoted, but the guy knew how to use his champions. He'd put the pressure on you. He'd tell you, "If you don't win the match tomorrow, Ed, you're not going east. I can't do anything for you if you don't win the match."

And I liked that. I'd say, "Don't worry about it, Mr. Jones."

Not all the players played by Jones' rules. Among his many run-ins were spats with Billie Jean King, Bobby Riggs, Darlene Hard and Pancho Gonzalez (who spelled it Gonzales in earlier days). This was in the L.A. Times obituary on Jones written by Jeff Prugh:

"He once clashed with Pancho Gonzales, then a teen-ager, and barred him from competition briefly. When his critics attacked him on grounds of Anglo prejudice, Mr. Jones heatedly denied the accusation."

" `All Richard (Pancho's given name) has to do is go back to school," he snapped. `We're not running a teen club for dropouts here.' "

> *Pat Yeomans* (L.A. Tennis Club historian): He wanted "his boys and girls" to be clean, neat and well mannered. He wanted them to write thank-you notes and be examples of good social training. He wanted them to be able to make speeches on the center court as well as play like tigers on the tennis court. His methods were Victorian. He was an example and a disciplinarian but he was personally involved with his youngsters. It was a crusade for "motherhood," country and the royal sport of tennis. He expected them to be able to share small talk with the Duchess of Kent, curtsey to Queen Elizabeth, to meet in the Rose Garden of the White House with the President. And they did.

So that was Perry T. Jones, benefactor and tyrant.

He was a tyrant with me at first. I was at the club for six months or so and I had a gal who was first in Southern California in the 15s. She was a Marlborough girl. Another mother came to me and said, "George, I heard Perry Jones proselytizing her mother to go take lessons from Bob Harmon." (He was a well-known coach in West L.A. and wrote some books, "Use Your Head in Tennis" and "Use Your Head in Doubles.")

I went home and told Miriam, "I'm going to walk into Jones' office tomorrow and I'm going to utter every damn word that I know." And she wisely said, "George, you're not going to do it, because if you're going to be a good coach, he's going to come to you. And if you're not, you don't deserve it anyway."

That's exactly what she told me. So I stuck with it and soon he was sending Harmon's students to me. Pretty soon I was driving him home, and whenever something came up, he'd get my advice.

For a number of years, he would organize the Perry Jones All-Stars to play against my USC players down at the Hotel del Coronado by San Diego. (Sometimes the All-Stars' matches were at the club or versus the Bruins at UCLA, but mostly in Coronado.) He would get the best players he could in Southern California – players the caliber of Herb Flam, who had been a star at UCLA, and Ed Yeomans, who had played at the University of North Carolina. He wanted to win. We won most of the time, but the All-Stars won some of the matches, too.

It was a great week when it was at Coronado because they had a lot of other tournaments going – father and son, mother and daughter and all that sort of thing. Practically the whole L.A. Tennis Club was down there that week and there were cocktail parties all over the place. Most of the rooms were right above the courts, so people could be at a party and look right down at their friends playing.

Members at the L.A. Tennis Club were very generous with the facilities, as far as top players and USC players were concerned. Every top player in the country could come there and be welcomed. There was plenty of room and the members were magnanimous about it.

One Sunday it got to be about 2 o'clock. Usually there were some matches organized among the players, but nothing had happened, they were just sitting around playing cards. So I figured maybe I'd get them in a round-robin with club members and cement our relations with the club better. So I brought it up to the guys and they were all for it.

I was playing and a girl pupil came running up and said, "Mr. Toley, do you know what you have out there playing?" I said, "No." She said, "You have eight players that have won at least one Grand Slam tournament!"

That's the way the club was in those days.

One of my ex-players, Ed Atkinson, reminded me of when Glen Petrovic came to America when he was in his late 20s. He thought he was good, and he was good. He had been one of the best European players, a champion. He went to the L.A. Tennis Club and Perry Jones lined him up with eight matches. Eight different guys – and he lost to all of them. Petrovic's son later played for me at USC.

For 38 years (1927-1973, 1981-1983), the biggest tournament in the West was played at the L.A. Tennis Club. In recent years, it has had many sites and names.* But lots of old-timers in Southern California call it by its old, honored moniker: the Pacific Southwest

---

    * Fountain Valley in Orange County, UCLA's Pauley Pavilion and now UCLA's outdoor complex and names such as Arco Pacific Southwest Open, Union 76 Pacific Southwest Tennis Open, Jack Kramer Open, Los Angeles Open, Volvo Tennis/ Los Angeles, Infiniti Open, Mercedes-Benz Cup, and ATP Countrywide Classic.

Championships. Or just the Pacific Southwest.

Wrote Ned Wheldon in *American Lawn Tennis* in 1939: "Always a favorite tournament for players of many lands after a grueling season of bitter competition, the Pacific Southwest nevertheless produces some of the finest tennis, for the holiday spirit, the friendly enthusiasm of the galleries and the trophies encrusted with famous names of champions of the last dozen years spur them on without the tension that so often mars important meetings. Southland society and the motion picture colony turned out en masse to cheer their guests and made their stay memorable with varied entertainment."

Show-biz celebrities have added to the charm from the beginning. Joe Bixler, longtime official of the Southern California Tennis Association, told *Tennis* magazine:

"Right from the first year, 1927, Hollywood celebrities were involved. Douglas Fairbanks, Mary Pickford, people like that. I remember watching an exhibition on center court with Mickey Rooney and Gilbert Roland playing against Errol Flynn and Charlie Chaplin. All the motion picture people had boxes on the west side of the stadium, in the front row, and the society people had their boxes at the south end. It really was the place to see and be seen. I think they all loved the tennis, but they were also interested in seeing each other."

I wasn't on hand at the start, but, according to the L.A. Times, the crowd at the inaugural Pacific Southwest included H.M. Haldeman, whose son was to be involved in the Watergate scandal with Richard Nixon; the Janss family, who built Westwood; William McAdoo, Secretary of State under President Woodrow Wilson; Harvey Mudd, who has a college in Claremont, Calif., named after him, plus actors Harold Lloyd and William Powell (who played Nick Charles in the celebrated "Thin Man" mystery movies).

"During the rest of the year, the Los Angeles Tennis Club looks much like any other good tennis club," said champion Alice Marble. "But for the championships it is decorated with colorful awnings which cover the entrance and tea garden; an extra stand is put up to accommodate the huge crowds – every box is filled – and a special one is erected on the center court for the honored guests."

I played in long pants, because of Perry Jones. He made us play in tailored, wool-gabardine trousers, and that wool gabardine really soaked up the moisture. Didn't wrinkle, but they got heavy with perspiration. Not only that, our shirts were wool jersey.

But you know what? It looked great on the court, it was a great uniform. In the early days, when you saw those guys in the wool-jersey shirts and tailored, wool-gabardine trousers, they looked just beautiful.

First of all, our trousers were tailor-made. We didn't have belts and they had pleats in the front, and they had darts in the back so they would fit you properly all around. And for the shirt to stay tucked in, we had two types. With one there was a rubber band inside your trousers to hold the shirt in; the shirt had an extension that went around your crotch.

Shorts, of course, were better and more comfortable. When I was out of Southern California, I wore shorts, but when I came home I had to wear trousers.

I was playing Bobby Riggs in the Pacific Southwest tournament one year – and, you know, Riggs and Perry Jones were not very friendly. Jones had to have him in the tournament because he was No. 1 in the world.

He didn't play in the tournament for about three years because Jones didn't invite him, but now he was 1, so Jones had to relent.

So Riggs came to me and said, "George, let's go out on the center court in shorts."

Well, if Jones saw you on center court in shorts, you didn't play. Or if girls didn't have dresses, they didn't get to appear. That was his rule. And of course, all white clothes. Long haircuts or beards — you didn't play, period.

I said, "Bobby, we're going to get out there and rally and we're going to be in our shorts and Perry Jones is going to stop us and make us get in our trousers." He said, "I'll tell you what we're going to do. Let's warm up on an outside court, and let's go and walk on the court and tell the officials we're ready to play."

That's what we did. And it probably was the first match in the history of the L.A. Tennis Club or the Pacific Southwest that was played in shorts. Jones didn't chew us out afterward either. I guess he didn't want to antagonize Riggs.

For the most part, I didn't care for teaching Hollywood people. But I gave lessons to actors Barbara Stanwyck and Robert Taylor. Vera-Ellen was a member of the L.A. Tennis Club. She was a really nice person. But actors and actresses were kind of temperamental. A producer who was a member of the club was a good friend of Katharine Hepburn's and he asked if I would go over to her house to give her lessons, and I said no. I was busy enough that I didn't have to.

I made friends with some. Peter Lorre and I were buddies. Peter was a great guy; he played at the Beverly Hills Tennis Club all the time. I always had trouble with him because I was the manager of the club and Monday morning at the beginning of each month, I had to come in and call all the business managers whose clients were behind in their dues. And Lorre was always behind, even though he was making $5,000 a week at that time.

I was always trying to gain weight, and Peter said, "George, I'll tell you one thing and I guarantee you'll gain weight." He wanted me to drink two jiggers of cream a day – pure cream. I said, "OK, Peter, I'll try it." It didn't make a bit of difference.

I gave lessons to Barbara Hutton, the heiress to the Woolworth fortune, for almost a year, five days a week at the Beverly Hills Tennis Club. Then she rented Doug Fairbanks' home in Pacific Palisades, so I had to go there. We'd play an hour or two of tennis, then she always had us for lunch. She always played in cashmere socks, and in the house the carpets were all white. When she married Cary Grant, they sent me a telegram telling me that they had eloped.

I gave him lessons, too. He could be a pill, and his coordination was terrible. We'd go to the court and Barbara would come to watch, and he would scream, "Barbara, you're not watching!" Which was ridiculous. Also, when we billed his office and were a couple of pennies off, we receive a notice about it. Just a couple of pennies!

We would have playing sessions at Barbara's place, then we'd have lunch and often Grant would drop me off at the Beverly Hills Tennis Club. On those rides he was reasonably good company.

Ozzie Nelson, the patriarch of the "Adventures of Ozzie and Harriet" family, came to the L.A. Tennis Club for a long time and took lessons. There is a quote posted at the club from Baron Pierre de Coubertin, founder of the modern Olympics: "The main issue in life is not the victory but the fight; the essential thing is not to have won but to have fought well." Ozzie was walking off the court one day, noticed the sign and said, "That was written by the runner-up." I used that on my players once in a while.

I taught Ricky Nelson, who couldn't play that often. He was the younger Nelson brother on the show and in real life and later was a hit-making singer until his death in a plane crash. Ricky was ranked No. 22 in the 15-and-under that year in Southern California and he decided to take the summer off from show business and ended up ranked No. 4 or 5. He was a good competitor and a good athlete; he could have been a good tennis player.

I was giving him lessons one day and he started to teach me about the game. So I said, "Ricky, you know so much about the game now, why don't we just stop lessons. Why waste your time and mine?" So that was it.

Dave, his older brother, was sitting on the bench by the court when it happened. Later he came into the pro shop and said, "Gosh, Mr. Toley, thank you for what you did. You know, he's doing the same thing on the set with my dad now."

Years afterward I ran into Ricky again. He was married by that time. Miriam and I and Katie were in Malibu in a restaurant. He was way across the room and he came hurrying over to say hello. He was very cordial even though I had stopped giving him lessons.

## TOLEY'S TIPS - 5

*KEEP IT SIMPLE – AT LEAST AT THE START:* The thing that always hit me in my education classes at USC was ``Go from the simple to the complex." Teaching has to be done that way. I always did simple things at first in repetition until they got it. When they didn't get it – whatever the lesson was – I would tell them, ``You didn't practice enough." If they said they had practiced, I would say, ``Well, let's just give it a little more time."

*GET A (LARGE) HANDLE:* I always wanted my pupils to use a racket handle as large as they could and still be comfortable. The reason is you're gripping more area on the handle, and in gripping more area you don't have to grip as tightly. I always taught people not to choke the racket, not to hold it tightly. The racket should be held loosely when you're waiting and then just before you go to hit the ball, firm it up a little.

This is especially important on the serve, because if you tighten up the grip, your wrist is locked and you can't snap your wrist and get your power.

*SHHHH:* Except for a sudden shriek or whistle or shout when it has been quiet, noise shouldn't bother a player. I'll give you an example. At the L.A. Tennis Club I taught on court 12, right across from the Black Foxe Military Academy (now defunct). The school had its band blaring at military parades in the afternoons. We weren't bothered. If you're concentrating on the court properly, you don't know noises occur.

# THOSE
# CHAMPIONSHIP SEASONS

Stan Smith
(Photo courtesy of the USC Sports Archives)

# THOSE CHAMPIONSHIP SEASONS

In 1954, Clark Cornell, a member of the L.A. Tennis Club, was president of the USC booster group called the Trojan Club. UCLA had just won two NCAA titles in a row. The Trojans had won the NCAA championship in 1946 (freshman Bob Falkenburg won singles and, with his brother Tom, doubles) and 1951 (Earl Cochell and Hugh Stewart won doubles) but had fallen behind the Bruins. We had only three tennis courts on campus and they were just atrocious – cracked surfaces, no backstops. Coach Lou Wheeler couldn't recruit championship-caliber players with facilities like that.

Clark sat me down and said, "George, we want you to be the SC tennis coach."

The last thing I needed was another job.

"No," I said. "I can't do both. I can't teach here at the club and run the tennis shop and be running from here over to SC. And I'm also teaching at Marlborough. No way."

"What I've been thinking of," he said, "is I'm going to talk to the club and see if we can get the program moved here. The players could be guest members and have their practices and matches here."

That's what happened. We practiced Mondays, Tuesdays, Thursdays and Fridays. We didn't practice Wednesdays because that was a busy day at the club, along with Saturdays and Sundays. All the doctors usually took off Wednesday afternoons.

It's a great club, and they treated those USC players well – we just had 19 years of bliss.

They loved the kids and the kids behaved well there. We never had any trouble. The rule was that any time there were no courts available and SC kids were on the courts, the kids would walk off. In the 19 years, I can only remember once when an SC kid was kicked off a court. Dennis Ralston was kicked off by a woman member. The president of the club, who was a J. Walter Thompson advertising executive, reamed her out good. Oh, he gave her hell.

I decided to take the job about a month before the 1954 season ended (Wheeler became the JV coach and we finished second to UCLA in the intercollegiates in Seattle). The pay was terrible. I think I got $600 a season, or at the most $900. In the later years, when I was getting $30 an hour teaching at the club, USC was paying me $22,000 a year. Miriam didn't want me to take it. Loyalty to the school was the only reason I did.

When I began recruiting late in the '54 season, everybody was locked in. UCLA had just got the three best juniors in the country, Mike Franks, Mike Green and Johnny Lesch.

I heard from somebody that Modesto Junior College had some boys from Mexico. I thought, "If nobody's recruited them by now, they couldn't be very good." But I had few choices.

So I was at the club one day and Bobby Perez was there, a former USC player (from the '51 title team) who spoke Spanish. I said, "Bob, I understand there's a boy at Modesto JC by the name of Contreras. He might be available. I don't know anything about him. Would you do me a favor and call up there and see if you can locate him?" He called and we had Pancho Contreras on the phone in about three minutes. And about three minutes later he agreed to come to USC.

It turned out his English was good. He was a brilliant kid anyway and later became president of North American Airlines in Mexico City, and head of public relations for Coca-Cola in Mexico City. But I'm getting ahead of my story.

Joaquin Reyes was with him, but he had to have another semester at Modesto. He came to USC a semester after Contreras. In doubles, they would serve and run up about halfway to the net, between the service line and the baseline, and stop. And their next step was backward, and their next step was to lob. That's the way they played until I went to work on them.

> *Ed Atkinson*: The first time Contreras and Reyes came to the L.A. Tennis Club to practice, Toley and Jacque Grigry played them some doubles. The Mexicans won the toss, Reyes went to serve, and when he was serving, Contreras was standing on the baseline. Toley said, "Wait a minute, hold everything." They said, "This is the way we play, coach, and we never lose." Toley said, "Fine, you guys play that way." And coach and Grigry beat them like 6-2, 6-1.

It's terrible to relinquish the net. It's bad enough in singles, but in doubles it's death. They were terrific athletes, but they were clueless. But George took those two guys and the next year they won the NCAA doubles.

They were our second team in 1955, but they won the intercollegiates. How they won it, though!

They played the favored team, from Texas, Sammy Giammalva and John Hernandez, on clay. We won the first set, they won the next two and then it rained. We got out the next day and they were leading 5-1 in the fourth, when Contreras sprained his ankle, got it caught in a fence. A doctor came down and said, "Well, the way that ankle is, I can fix it so he won't injure it more. But I'll have to wrap it like a cast practically."

He taped him up and somehow we went on to win it 15-13 in the fifth set. Contreras and Reyes withstood six match points against them. Not a bad start to USC's Latin American connection.

Contreras was a hard-working kid. At Modesto he worked in a hotel, washing dishes and making salads. For a while at SC he was a "hasher" – bus boy and dishwasher – at the Alpha Tau Omega fraternity. One semester at USC he was taking 17 units, earned a B-minus average despite still battling the language barrier, had a maintenance job on campus cleaning the courts, taught Spanish at the Berlitz Language Schools, played tennis five days a week and on Sundays played for a Latin-American soccer team. He had no car, so to get to the L.A. Tennis Club, he took a bus to Hollywood Boulevard and walked two blocks to the grounds, lugging his rackets.

That year the NCAA tournament was at North Carolina – on clay, as I said. Texas had Giammalva, who played Davis Cup for the U.S. And my No. 1 singles man, Jacque Grigry, had never won a match on clay. The tournament before the NCAA's, he had lost to Texas' No. 4 man.

On cement, Grigry was greased lightning. He was a volleyer, a net-rusher and he moved great. On cement he had the traction he couldn't have on clay. I told him that at the NCAA's he was not going to net. I kept nagging him and trying to convince him. His eyes weren't good and he couldn't pick up the ball fast enough to rush the net and volley on clay. Finally it got through to him that he should stay back. Then I had to think about his forehand, which was terrible.

"Jacque," I said, "It doesn't matter if your forehand is weak, because they can't put the ball away on you like they can on a fast court. You don't have to worry, just hit your forehand down the middle. Just wait for your consistent backhand."

He got to the semifinals for us against José Aguero of Tulane, who won the tournament singles. That and the doubles play of Contreras and Reyes won the championship for us.

Alejandro "Alex" Olmedo — sometimes called "The Chief" because of his Inca blood — came to America from Peru in 1953 or early in 1954 and he hadn't finished high school. His father was an employee at a tennis club in Arequipa. An ex-Bruin, Stan Singer, had gone to Peru to develop athletes and discovered this talented kid and encouraged him. Alex lived for a while in the Singer family home in Lima. Singer sent him to California to see then-USC coach Lou Wheeler, who had been Singer's coach at Marshall High in L.A.

(Olmedo had had a brief international debut in 1951, losing out in his first match at Forest Hills, to USC's Jacque Grigry 6-4, 6-0, 6-1.)

Olmedo spent about a year here and then one day, during the Pacific Southwest, I was out in front of my tennis shop talking with him, and he said, "George, I have to leave the United States and go to Mexico to live. My visitor's visa is up and I have to leave." We'd been trying to get him to go to college, but he didn't want to go, he just wanted to play tennis.

"Well, Alex," I said, "there's one possibility you can stay here. You can stay with a student visa if you want to go to school." I sent him to Modesto JC and they got him in, and later he transferred to USC. If I hadn't been out in front of the tennis shop that day, he'd have been gone to Mexico.

When Alex came to L.A., he was behind boys his age. Even after he'd been here a year, playing a lot at Poinsettia Park, he was behind, because when I sent him up to Modesto, he was third on that team, and the two men ahead of him were just out of the juniors. One had won the national juniors and the other was Mike Green, a top junior who went on to UCLA. But Alex caught up quickly.

> *Alex Olmedo*: George was great to me. He was a coach, he was a friend, a guy who has guided me through my life.
>
> In order to become a world-class player, you have to be able to control the serve to such a degree that you can pinpoint it. Both serves. He had me practicing on a back court by the hour. "OK, there's nobody to play now. Take a basket and go practice your serve." We jumped rope, got in shape, worked on the backhand, too. He tried to teach me a topspin backhand. I wish I would have done it better.

"The Chief worked out with George every day, often for several hours at a time," said World Tennis magazine. "The exaggerated slice on his backhand disappeared, the volley backswing shortened, his first serve calmed down, and he developed more spin and depth on his second serve. The greatest improvement was seen in the growth of tactical sense. He learned to play percentage tennis in speed and direction, to analyze his opponents and to exploit this knowledge."

Tennis All-America teams began in 1957, and Alex was on the initial two first teams. He was NCAA singles champion in 1956 and 1958 and NCAA doubles champ in 1956 (with Contreras) and 1958 (with Ed Atkinson). He probably would have been the singles champ in 1957, too, but USC was on probation because of violations by the football staff. Even as young as he was, in 1959 he won the singles at Wimbledon and the Australian Open.

What I remember most vividly — even though I wasn't there and had to follow the results through the news media — is Alex's Davis Cup play in Australia late in December of 1958. Perry T. Jones was the nonplaying captain of the U.S. team and picked Ham Richardson, Barry MacKay, Chris Crawford, 18-year-old Earl "Butch" Buchholz and noncitizen Olmedo. Such a thing had not been done before by America, but Alex qualified because he had been a U.S. resident for more than three years and had not played Davis Cup for any other country. In fact, Peru did not have a team and agreed to the arrangement "with pleasure." Alex had to agree to return later to USC to complete his education. (Aussie Marty Mulligan played for Italy, Aussie Bob Hewitt played for South Africa, ex-USC player Bob Falkenburg of Los Angeles played for Brazil.)

The team was selected in October. The same month, Olmedo and Richardson, who had been NCAA singles champion for Tulane in 1954, were sent by the U.S. Tennis Association to the Philippines, Hong Kong and Japan for exhibitions. Then they hooked up with the rest of the team in Sydney in mid-November and played in tournaments there, Melbourne and Perth.

Jack Kramer, in Australia as a consultant for Jones,

was by then the world's big-time pro tennis promoter and a controversial figure Down Under. People there, including I believe Aussie captain Harry Hopman, accused him of wanting to become czar of the sport. Kramer said he merely wanted to be the czar of the professional branch, and Jones defended him.

There was also controversy within the team, and Kramer was part of that. Richardson, ranked No. 1 in America ahead of Olmedo at No. 2 and MacKay at No. 3, was a diabetic and had to withdraw from a tournament in late November-early December because of that disease.

The Davis Cup matches were played in Brisbane, and there Kramer told reporters, "I doubt if we can win by playing him (Richardson) in both the singles and doubles." Ham was angry over this and replied, according to the Associated Press, "I feel wonderful. I am playing the best tennis of my life. I feel I am the best player and that our best chance of winning the Cup depends on my playing all three days."

"I am not obligated to anybody," Jones told reporters. "My only obligation is to try to win the Cup with the best men available."

Winning the Davis Cup was a big deal, especially that year because since Hopman had taken the reins in 1950, Australia had beaten the U.S. in seven of eight challenge rounds.*

America was a huge underdog. Australia was thought to be invincible because it had Ashley Cooper, who had

---

* Remember that until 1972, the defending-champion nation happily waited until all the challengers battled through a tournament for the right to try for the crown in a challenge round. Since then, the champion country has to play through the draw..

that year won the singles championships of Australia, Great Britain (Wimbledon) and the U.S.; Mal Anderson, U.S. 1957 champion and 1958 U.S. finalist, and Neale Fraser, 1958 Wimbledon finalist.

Jones picked Olmedo and MacKay to play singles, and Richardson did not take it well, saying — some would call it whining — "Mr. Jones has been most unfair to me and to the rest of the team. He did not have the courtesy, much less the courage, to tell me I would not play. Instead, I had to learn of this decision by telephone from a newspaper (reporter)."

Milton Stadium in Brisbane was a quagmire for the opening singles matches that day late in December. A canvas covering the court had failed to fend off a night-long tropical rainstorm. Olmedo and Anderson both put on spikes after the slipping, sliding first two games. Olmedo stunned the capacity crowd of more than 18,500 by defeating Anderson 8-6, 2-6, 9-7, 8-6. In the third set, Anderson got to set point five times but couldn't cash in.

"It was a great comeback by the young Peruvian," said the AP, "and the crowd stood as one on this humid day and cheered him as though he were one of their own."

Then Cooper defeated MacKay 4-6, 6-3, 6-2, 6-4 to even the score. Richardson, perhaps somewhat over his disgust, played doubles with Olmedo and they beat Anderson and Fraser 10-12, 3-6, 16-14, 6-3, 7-5 – 82 games, a record for final-round doubles. Ed Atkinson told me he listened to that match on the radio and was sure after the first two sets that Ham and Alex were dead meat. So did I.

On the decisive day, Anderson beat MacKay 7-5, 13-11, 11-9, leaving it all up to world No. 1 Cooper vs. Olmedo. Alex clinched the victory for America – and a huge amount of publicity and good will for himself – by beating Cooper 6-3, 4-6, 6-4, 8-6. The AP called it "the biggest upset in the history of the competition."

Maybe Richardson should have played instead of MacKay, but Jones certainly made the correct choice in going with Olmedo.

Alex won not because he was the best tennis player but because he was the best athlete. It had rained and they had to play on wet courts, so they used spikes. And if you're playing on a grass court and have to adjust to the wetness and wearing spikes, athleticism is an issue. Movement is entirely different. Alex could adapt better, cover the net better with spikes on a wet court.

> *Alex Olmedo:* I finished my college eligibility, then in '59 I was going to school and I was winning every major tournament. Jack Kramer approached me and he said, "Well, if you turn pro, we can give you such-and-such amount of money." I had never seen money. ... I said, "Hell, I'll turn pro." I talked to George and he said, "Finish the school year and then you can turn pro the end of the year."
>
> The 1959-60 tour was Pancho Gonzalez, Ken Rosewall, Tony Trabert and myself, in a round-robin. Pancho Segura replaced Trabert along the way. Kramer put in a new gimmick, the three-bounce rule. Gonzalez had the best serve in professional tennis. I had the best serve in amateur tennis. His rule meant that you served – that's one bounce on the court. The return you had to let bounce – that's two bounces. The return of the return had to bounce before a man could finally come to the net.
>
> So we found ourselves awfully confused. Gonzalez won the tour.

In 1960, another great Latin American player came

to USC – Rafael Osuna. For two years my Mexican players had been telling me about him, saying he was the best prospect they had ever had. He was a good all-around athlete, playing soccer and basketball as well as tennis. Later he told me that one of the reasons he didn't concentrate on tennis was that if he did he knew he'd go to USC. And he didn't want to leave his family in Mexico City.

The semester had already started when I got a call from Yves Lemaitre, a Mexican who had played for Modesto JC and then for me in '56 and '57. He said Rafe had decided to come. It was a hassle getting him a visa and getting him through customs, and at first he took just English, nothing toward a degree. He was an introvert, but his personality soon blossomed.

> *Ed Atkinson:* When Osuna came, I said to myself, "This poor guy. He thinks he's going to hook onto the Olmedo train." His IQ was probably 160; the guy was really something. His father was like a chess champion in Mexico. The day before Rafe died, he beat his father in chess for the first time.
>
> We used to have to chin ourselves. He couldn't do one chin-up. He was weak. He couldn't serve hard, he couldn't hit the ball hard. Alex at least had that big serve, even when he was getting off the banana boat. But Osuna couldn't break an egg. But he had the heart of a lion and tremendous ground strokes.

Everything Osuna did on the court was bad fundamentally, in part because he was such a natural. He had great hand-eye coordination and quickness, so he could get away with bad footwork against lesser competition. He didn't bother to get into position for his strokes, which, despite what Ed Atkinson remembers, were all bad. He was real flippy and he took long strokes on his volleys. We had to tear his game apart, start him like he was beginning tennis.

He had had no success to speak of in the sport. He was ranked 10th in Mexico, because he was more into basketball and soccer. So I had him on the ball machine all semester, and he just worked by the hour, worked on stroking the ball, worked on getting his feet into position.

*Rafael Belmar Osuna* (USC letterman 1986; Rafael Osuna's nephew): When my uncle first started working out with coach, and coach had to make a lot of modifications to his game, they would get up early, meet at the L.A. Tennis Club and coach would tell Rafael what to do. And then coach would go over to his teaching court to give some lessons.

Coach was tight timewise because he was trying to get in as many lessons as possible. When coach was through prior to his lunch hour starting, my uncle came to his court and asked, "Coach, can you see if I'm doing it correctly?" My uncle started hitting some serves and coach noticed some significant progress. So he stayed on for a little while.

When the balls in the basket were all used, my uncle sprinted to pick them up – in a full sprint, picking up the scattered balls and bring them back to the baseline. So coach stuck around and said, "We'll do one more basket." After the second basket was used, my uncle kept sprinting to gather the balls, and coach said to himself, "I'm going to see how far this guy is going to carry this." Well, the guy didn't stop. Every time the basket was used up, my uncle would sprint to pick up the balls.

Coach said, "I stuck around, worked on his serve, so I didn't get lunch."

But it was worth it to coach.

When that summer came, the Mexican association was willing to foot Osuna's bill to play tennis and go to Wimbledon with the rest of them, and I talked him into not going. I said, "You've worked hard all these months, Rafe. You're going to get out on the tennis court and tear it all apart. You're going to hearken back to your old habits; it's bound to happen. I think you ought to stay here. Stay this summer and practice and you'll really ground what you've done, whereas you'll take a chance going back East to revert to what you were doing."

And that's what he did.

I always told my kids when they had to make a change that every time they hit the ball with their old habit, they had to hit the ball 10 times with the new habit to make up for it.

Osuna did something when he arrived that no other player I'd coached had done – he head-faked when he volleyed. He thought that was a clever thing. He planned to volley to the left, but he looked right because he wanted the opponent to run to the right. You just don't do those things in tennis. You have enough trouble just hitting the ball looking at it without head-faking somebody.

All you have to do is head-fake a couple of times and the top players will nail it anyway.

Osuna always had a natural backhand volley, but on his forehand volley he would always stroke it, take too big a swing. At the end of the summer going into his senior year, I said, "Rafe, you're just going to work on the forehand volley." I had him bring his racket back just so far and stop it, and he did that for two months.

Not move his arm at all – just with his wrist action. His forehand volley became equal to his backhand volley. And he forgot all about those head fakes.

Rafe always did everything I told him, never questioned me. His sophomore year, he played Allen Fox of UCLA in the final of the Valley Hunt Club tournament in Pasadena — the Southern California Intercollegiates it was called. He lost because his backhand was just a slice. It wasn't adequate.

"You can't break serve that way," I told him. "You have to have more aggression. You have to get a topspin backhand. I don't care if you lose every match for the rest of the season, I want you to use a topspin backhand every time."

So he stuck by it. A couple of months later, against a Stanford man, he lost the first set but won the second and third sets easily. The backhand had jelled. And about three weeks later, the Ojai tournament was on. He beat Fox in the final in straight sets, losing HIS serve three times. That means he had to break serve five times. He lost some matches at the beginning using the topspin backhand, but he stuck with it and that's the kind of kid he was.

He had great confidence in himself, great confidence.

USC didn't just have Latins on the team, not with California such a rich source of talent. With Dennis Ralston, I never did any recruiting. We hardly ever talked about it when he was down at the club from Bakersfield. He had gone to Australia before he entered college, because the USTA put him on the Davis Cup team for grooming, and Australia was the holder, so he went there as an alternate. At the time, Chuck McKinley was also traveling and tried very hard to recruit him to Trinity, in San Antonio, Texas.

At the Southern Cal tournament in May of 1960, I was working in the shop rather late one night and Denny was walking by and I hailed him and asked him if he had made up his mind what to do. He said, "Yeah, I think I have. I might as well tell you now. I am coming to SC."

It was either that day or the next that he told me he was going to Wimbledon. I knew that Rafe Osuna was going also and I asked, "Would you like to play doubles with him?" "That would be fabulous," he said. "Let me check with (Perry) Jones first," because naturally he'd have to. And they played Wimbledon doubles together, even though neither had ever played a college match (we hadn't played Rafe as a freshman). Of course, I wanted that to happen because it would jell the landing of Ralston a little more for me.

Well, those young Trojan varsity-players-to-be won the doubles on that famous Centre Court, beating Mike Davies and Bobby Wilson in the final. And they had been down a match point in a qualifying match. (Rafe won again in 1963, with countryman Antonio Palafox. Ralston got to the doubles final one more time, with Arthur Ashe in 1971, but lost to Roy Emerson and Rod Laver.)

That same summer, Ramsey Earnhart, a top player from Ventura, Calif., was going east to play the circuit. He always had forehand problems. He choked like mad on the forehand.

So I advised him to "go out with the idea that you're going to miss forehands, that you KNOW you choke on it. So don't try to make them all. Just hit it. If you miss, think, `Well, I'm supposed to miss it.' Just bunch a couple together, or maybe make one and break serve and that's all you need anyway."

Because Ramsey was great at holding serve. He was a fine volleyer, had a fine serve, a great overhead. He was a net player, period, because he had to be since he couldn't depend on that forehand. He had to get the hell away from that baseline.

He made 11th in the country on that one little thing. He came back and we talked about it and he said, "God, what a difference. I'd miss the ball and I didn't give a darn. So when the next ball came, I had a chance of making it."

I believe that in 1963 we had the greatest college tennis team ever. There is a photograph of it in a display at the Collegiate Hall of Fame in Athens, Ga. That team hasn't been surpassed; not even close.

First of all, that year our No. 2 player, Osuna, was ranked No. 1 in the world. Our No. 1 player, Ralston, was ranked No. 7 in the world. They had been the Wimbledon doubles champions in 1960. That summer, Osuna would be Wimbledon doubles champ again, with countryman Antonio Palafox, and Forest Hills singles champ, beating Frank Froehling III in the final. Ralston would be on our championship Davis Cup team, winning two matches in the challenge round vs. Australia. At Adelaide, he would beat John Newcombe in five sets and join with Chuck McKinley to beat Roy Emerson and Neale Fraser.

Tom Edlefsen was No. 3 and ranked ninth in the country. He hit the ball very hard. Big serve. Everybody on that team was a great big hitter. Every guy. Tom was a San Francisco kid from junior college and he contacted me and said he wanted to come. I can remember that when I got the OK from our admissions office, I called him and he screamed in joy.

*Tom Edlefsen* (USC letterman 1963-65-66): I'd been

out of tennis for two years. I'd been in a high school in Pennsylvania for two and I hadn't touched a racket. I went to USC when I was 20 and I hadn't played for two solid years. I was raw. I had played that summer, but I wasn't anything like I was going to be after he got hold of me for a year.

I think Toley has forgotten more than any coach knows today. I'm sure he has forgotten more.

Edlefsen's movement on the volley was about as bad as you could get. He would run up and stop dead about two or three steps back of the service line and then try to start again. Just atrocious.

All the good volleyers lunge. Side to side, a sort of lunge or leap. The way I taught it, I would place the player at the net in the middle of the court and then I would hit a ball right down the line to one side or the other. They would take one step and lunge. And they could cover almost any ball down the line with just one step and a lunge.

I was afraid Edlefsen would hurt himself learning to lunge, because he had never done anything like that. I took a net and we went down to the beach to a volleyball court and put the tennis net up. I put him at the net in the middle and I would hit balls down the lines and he learned to lunge, falling in the sand if need be. He learned it and became a good enough volleyer to win the Pacific Southwest doubles with Bill Bond in 1963, beating 1963 Wimbledon champs Osuna and Palafox.

Bond and Ramsey Earnhart alternated at No. 4. Bond was an honor student, the son of the pro at the La Jolla Beach & Tennis Club. He was a first-team All-America the season before, had won the Irish singles in 1961 and would eventually make it into the Intercollegiate Tennis Hall of Fame. Earnhart was a returning two-year, first-team All-America, and had won NCAA doubles two years in a row with Osuna.

No. 6 man Chuck Rombeau, a lefty, was anything but a slouch. He had been the state junior college champion and had a win over Ralston in the juniors. As good a sixth player as any college has ever had.

Get this, we were so strong and so deep that our third doubles team was Rombeau and Earnhart – and Earnhart had not only won two NCAA titles with Osuna but had twice been a semifinalist in the NCAA singles.

UCLA was also talented and deep in the '63 season, with Arthur Ashe, Charlie Pasarell, Paul Palmer and David Reed, all of whom were to make the All-America team that year or had done so previously. Plus they had Dave Sanderlin, who would be an All-America in 1964, and a top kid from Scandinavia, Thorvald Moe, who at No. 6 was awfully strong.

Something unusual happened before the first time we played the Bruins that year. The chairman of a tournament in Houston wanted Osuna and Ralston down there to play Chuck McKinley and Frank Froehling. The event had top Australians but needed some U.S. players. I thought it was risky to have my two best players go down there and play on clay and then zip right back and play against UCLA, but the boys wanted to go and kept hounding me. They flew down there on Saturday and played a sort of Davis Cup-type exhibition on Sunday. They played in the tournament until Friday and flew home. I got them on the court at UCLA to get used to competing on cement again.

Osuna lost a long match to Pasarell, but Ralston easily made the difficult transition from clay to cement and beat Ashe. We won 6-3.

But the amazing thing was that in the rematch at the L.A. Tennis Club, we beat that outstanding Bruin team 9-0! Here are the scores:

Ralston def. Pasarell 6-3, 9-7.

Osuna def. Ashe 6-2, 6-4.

Edlefsen def. Reed 11-9, 6-4.

Earnhart def. Sanderlin 6-2, 2-6, 6-2.

Bond def. Palmer 4-6, 6-3, 6-3.

Rombeau def. Moe 3-6, 6-1, 6-2.

Osuna/Ralston def. Ashe/Pasarell 6-4, 6-2.

Bond/Edlefsen def. Palmer/Reed 4-6, 6-1, 11-9.

Earnhart/Rombeau def. Moe/Sanderlin 12-10, 6-2.

The NCAA tournament was in Princeton, N.J., and Princeton graduate Frank Deford wrote this about it for *Sports Illustrated*:

"The team from the University of Southern California not only is the best college tennis team in the world today but probably the best in history. Its top man is U.S. Davis Cupper Dennis Ralston, U.S. doubles champion in 1961 and still only a Trojan junior. He won the singles impressively. One of his teammates was Mexican Davis Cupper Rafael Osuna. They needed five sets to win the doubles, but the team they beat — Ramsey Earnhart and Bill Bond — also were Trojans and probably the second best doubles team in the country." (Ramsey and Bill beat Dennis and Rafael in the conference final.)

We clinched the title on Thursday, with two days of play remaining. "We were the best players in the country," Earnhart has said.*

---

* He became tennis director and coach at the Idle Hour Country Club in Macon, Georgia. Ralston became tennis director at

at the Broadmoor resort in Colorado Springs, after being U.S. Davis Cup captain, a pioneering pro and men's tennis coach at Southern Methodist. Bond has for years run the tennis program at the La Jolla Beach & Tennis Club. Ralston is teacing in the Palm Springs area. Ralston, Osuna, Bond, Earnhart and Edlefsen are in the Intercollegiate Tennis Hall of Fame in Athens, Georgia. Rombeau  died young in the early 1970s, of a brain tumor.

Osuna won four majors, the 1963 U.S. singles, 1962 U.S. doubles and the 1960 and 1963 Wimbledon doubles. He was a member of Mexico's Davis Cup team for 11 years. With Vincent Zarazua, he won the Olympic Games doubles in 1968. He was ranked No. 1 in the world in 1963, as I have said. He became a Phillip Morris executive in Mexico and had a wonderful life going, but he died young. As I understand it, he was scheduled for a flight in Mexico on a Friday in June, 1969, but it came up that he had to meet the president of Mexico. So he got the last seat on an earlier flight and it crashed in the mountains near Monterey. All 79 people on board were killed. He was 30 years old and left his wife, Leslie, and his son, Rafe Jr. World Tennis magazine called him "one of the best loved men that tennis has ever known."

Loved most of all, of course, in his homeland. After his Wimbledon doubles victory in 1960, he returned to Mexico transformed from a relative nobody to a superstar. Mexico met the U.S. in Davis Cup action at Centro Deportivo Chapultepec in Mexico City, adjacent to Chapultepec Park. Osuna was running late for his match because he stopped to give autographs to a throng of kids outside the club. Officials told him, "Rafael, if you don't come in, they're going to default you." Olmedo answered, "You see all these kids? They're my sons. If they don't come in, I don't come in." They had to open the gates and let the kids in for free. He beat America's Barry MacKay 3-6, 8-6, 6-4, 6-4. According to Rafe's nephew, kids got in for free when he played.

An award is given each year to an NCAA male tennis player who has demonstrated competitive excellence and sportsmanship and has made contributions to the sport. It is called the Rafael H. Osuna Memorial Trophy, and rightly so. The first winner, in 1969, was USC's and Mexico's Joaquin Loyo-Mayo, which was terrific because Osuna paid Loyo-

The Trojans of 1963 not only were great players, great guys and great friends. There was wonderful camaraderie on that team. For instance, the previous year in Mexico City, the Mexican Davis Cup team beat the U.S. and the crowd went wild. Osuna kept trying to fight his way through the admirers to get to Ralston and console him.

*Tom Edfelsen*: We played up in Seattle one time in a tournament. We bet Osuna that he couldn't run in the nude past the elevator door and get a Coke from a machine on the other side and get back to the room before the elevator door opened. Little did he know that we would lock him out. Because he was Mexican and they don't play those kind of games down there. But we did. He was locked out in the hall with no clothes, pounding on the door.

It was a tight-knit group. Just to give you an example, after college I was in the Air Force and some immunization serum knocked me out for a year. I was in the hospital, paralyzed. I couldn't move anything. And before even my parents knew I was sick, guess who calls me on the telephone? I got a call from Dennis and Charlie Rombeau and a couple of other guys. Dennis is one of the most thoughtful people I ever met — I have the fondest memories of him doing that type of thing.

I'll give you another illustration of how close we were. Ralston, myself, Rombeau and Bond had an apartment together. We got along fine. Rombeau did all the cooking. Steak and potatoes, that's all we had.

---

Mayo's tuition when the youngster first went to L.A. to learn English.

That summer, after Osuna won the U.S. championship at Forest Hills, beating Froehling 7-5, 6-4, 6-2. I wrote him this letter:

"Dear Rafe,

"It is hard for me to express in words how proud I am of you and of your great triumph. Your friends from Los Angeles feel the same. You can't imagine how many people have called me or have come to see me to give me their congratulations! Their sincerity shines out when they voice their opinion about you – not only as an athlete, but also as a human being. You should be very proud because you have earned it with your daily struggle, in the most tenacious and persevering way.

"If the euphoria was big here, I can't imagine the excitement in Mexico when they knew that they had conquered their first Forest Hills championship! I would love to have seen the boys' happy faces. (Yves, Pancho, Joaquin, Eduardo.)

"And, of course, your parents: they sent me a beautiful telegram that I shall exhibit, with great pride, on the club's billboard. They congratulate me for `my' triumph – and I understand, as a father, what they tell me: `The success of Rafael compensates, in a small way, for the sorrow of him being away from home. ... '

"I am very happy that you have given this great satisfaction to your country, to your parents, and to all the people who love you. Rafe, I was deeply moved when I talked to you, and was aware of your excitement when you called right after you had won the tournament. ...

Sincerely,<br>George"

*Dick Leach:* In 1968, Rafe, my former teammate and good friend, asked me to play doubles at La Jolla in the National Hardcourt Doubles Championship. What an experience for me! In the quarterfinals, we played Tom Gorman and Stan Smith. I couldn't buy a return on Stan's serve, it was so big. So Rafe said he would shake Stan up by returning his serve from the service line! Rafe was hitting half-volley winners off Stan's big first serve, from the service line. Stan got so shook up he started trying to hit Rafe with his first serve.

In the final we played his two Mexican Davis Cup teammates, Marcelo Lara and Joaquin Loyo-Mayo (also SC guys). Here I am on the court with three very quick Mexicans. I said, "Rafe, what are we going to do?" He said, "No worries. I know their choking point is $50 cash and last night I bet them each $100 on the match." At one point in the match, I hit a good first serve and won the point, and he got mad at me. Rafe said, "Serve easier so I can poach and get them pissed off."

In 1969, just before his horrible accident, I played against Rafe at the old Pacific Southwest Tennis Championships. Rafe had basically retired and was only playing because he was in L.A. on business. They gave him a pick-up partner from Jamaica, Richard Russell. We were all at the net for the spin for serve and Russell asked Osuna which side he wanted to play, forehand or backhand. In the greatest reply I have ever heard, Rafe said, "I won Wimbledon on the forehand side with Ralston and on the backhand side with Antonio Palafox. So I guess it doesn't really matter which side I play. How about you?"

I shouldn't confess to this, but I will. In the 1964 NCAA

Tournament, I didn't see the championship-deciding doubles match between Ashe and Pasarell of UCLA and our Bond and Ralston.

It had been close between us and the Bruins all season. In the first dual match, at Westwood, they won the deciding third doubles. In the rematch at the L.A. Tennis Club, we won the deciding third doubles. At the conference, same thing – we won the deciding last doubles.

So on to East Lansing, Mich., and the NCAA Tournament. My guys were great, always loyal to USC. They always played the intercollegiates. They never asked me to skip the NCAA Tournament to play at Wimbledon. Never did I hear, "Coach, any chance that we can skip the NCAA's and play Wimbledon?" They would have had to be in Europe a week or two in advance to practice on grass. Chuck McKinley never played in the intercollegiates all the four years he was at Trinity. He always got to go to Wimbledon.

I always tried to get them to Wimbledon as quickly as I could after the NCAA's. I usually thought, "There's no way these guys can do anything over there."

That year, when top seed Ralston played Big Ten champion Marty Riessen of Northwestern in the NCAA final, the match went lickety-split, with Denny winning 6-4, 6-4, 6-1. There was heckling from the pro-Riessen crowd and at one point Denny yelled "Quiet!" at a fan. The way he wielded his racket did a better job at quieting the hecklers than any comment he could make.

Anyway, I told Denny's wife, Linda, that maybe, despite the length of the tournament, he could make the scheduled flight to England. She said, "But coach, we haven't packed." I said, "Linda, let's go." Michigan

State coach Stan Drobac gave us a great Oldsmobile convertible. Linda and I raced back to the hotel, packed in a hurry, grabbed Bond's luggage, and drove back to the stadium.

As we came back, cars were leaving the stadium. We called out, "Who won? Who won?" "Oh, USC," they told us.

It turned out that Bond and Ralston had won in straight sets, 6-2, 6-3, 6-4, to give USC its third straight national tennis title, 26-25. UCLA's doubles tactics were never very good and I just knew we were going to win that match. I didn't have to be there. That's the way I felt. And it was so important for me to get Ralston and Bond off to Wimbledon as early as possible, because they'd been such great kids.

In a 1964 autograph book given me by the team, Ralston wrote, "You're a fine coach and a fine person. I appreciate all your assistance and I wish you and all the coming SC teams all the best. I also want to thank you for the poker lessons and gin (rummy) advice." He didn't mention the quick trip to the Lansing airport.

That was the golden age of college tennis. In 1963, as I mentioned before, when Osuna was a senior and Ralston a junior, they ended up ranked Nos. 1 and 7 in the world. Trinity University's Chuck McKinley was No. 2 and won Wimbledon singles. The next year McKinley and Ralston, still undergraduates into June, were Nos. 5 and 9. In the year-ending U.S. rankings for 1963, McKinley, Ralston, Marty Riessen of Northwestern, Arthur Ashe of UCLA, our Tom Edlefsen and UCLA's Charles Pasarell were Nos. 1, 2, 5, 6, 9 and 10. In 1964, Ralston, McKinley and Ashe were 1-2-3.

Edlefsen stayed with us a few more seasons. We won our eighth NCAA title in 1966, when we outscored

UCLA 27-23 at Coral Gables, Florida. Stan Smith was runner-up in singles (losing to UCLA's Pasarell), Tom was a semifinalist and Jerry Cromwell made the quarters.

The gold faded somewhat after that, but college tennis remained at a high level. Smith, USC '68, was ranked No. 7 in America at the end of 1967 and No. 3 at the end of 1968. One year out of school he was No. 1.

Smith won more national and international titles than any other player I've coached, but I didn't commit to him until June, which is late. I'll tell you why. There was a South African, Ray Moore, 17 years old. He was beating top players on the circuit and he was definitely, at that time, a better prospect than Smith. A great guy, and I think he would have won the intercollegiates more than Stan, who won it once. Moore was thinking of coming, but his national association stepped in with sponsoring help, so he could just concentrate on tennis.

That's the only opening I had, so if I had given it to Moore, Smith probably would have gone to UCLA. The Bruins were recruiting him. But Stan came to USC and it worked out pretty well for both of us and the school, I'd say. (These days, Moore helps Charlie Pasarell run a top tournament in Indian Wells, near Palm Springs.)

Stan, a lean 6-foot-3, is sometimes described as having been a clumsy donkey as a kid, not even agile enough to be a ball boy. But I first saw him play when he was 16 and he never looked that clumsy to me. He obviously was coordinated or he would not have been able to play on a very good Pasadena High basketball team.

> *Stan Smith* (USC letterman 1966-67-68): I was 17 years old and there was a Davis Cup match between the U.S. and Mexico at the L.A. Tennis Club. The

person in charge of ball boys thought I was too big and clumsy and might bother the players, who included Dennis Ralston and Rafael Osuna.

Quitting the Pasadena basketball team to concentrate on tennis was the hardest decision I had ever made up to that time. Coach George Terzian, who was a tennis player, said that I could play tennis one day a week and then on weekends during the basketball season. I did that for about a month, then said I needed more tennis. He said that I could play two days a week and weekends. I tried that and my basketball suffered and I still wasn't playing as much tennis as I and others thought I should be.

After about two or three months, I quit basketball. Without me, a starter who would have contributed down the stretch, it went to the semifinals of the section. Jim Marsh and Bill Sweek, who went to on to play at USC and UCLA, were on that team. The guys on the team were not happy, but I did improve my tennis, driving to the L.A. Tennis Club every day after school.

The Pasadena Tennis Patrons wanted Stan to go to USC and Perry Jones pleaded his case with me. He won the Southern California 18s in May and looked like a good prospect for tennis, but there was one peculiarity about him. He was stiff as a board, not limber at all. But a great kid who worked hard. He didn't move that stiffly, it was just in his strokes.

In his senior year of high school, when he quit basketball so that he could work out regularly at the club, the Southern California Tennis Association paid me to work on his strokes, especially his forehand volley.

Freshmen couldn't play with the varsity in those years, but Smith hit every day with a classmate from Mexico,

Joaquin Loyo-Mayo, a left-hander. Stan credited that experience with helping him in later years against the likes of Rod Laver, Tony Roche and Ian Crookenden.

As I recollect, in my own early tennis, I didn't hit the ball square, didn't use what players call the "sweet spot." I worked at it, concentrated hard, made it a big project and solved the problem. Well, Smith didn't have that feel at all and never developed it. One day he came to me and said, "Coach, I'm having trouble serving." We got a basket of balls and went down to the court and I said, "Serve some." He started to serve and mis-hit the ball. I didn't say anything and waited and waited and waited. I wanted to see if he could figure out what he was doing wrong. He served about 30 balls and had no idea of what was wrong – he was not hitting the sweet spot! He didn't know it. So I told him, "Make sure you're guiding the middle of that racket to the ball. Just think about it more."

It turned out he always wore out the fourth string from the top of his racket. That's very high. If you hit the ball there, the racket — and the stroke — don't have all the faculties that they should have — the power or anything. It took us a long time until we finally got the ball on his serve down to the middle of the racket.

Bob Lutz, another of our great stars at USC, started at Stanford and transferred to USC midway through his freshman year (1965-66). Smith, who had played doubles with Lutz in the juniors, was pleased that they could be reunited and wasn't overly concerned about who would play No. 1 in singles.

I never had to split up my top two players to make my doubles stronger. We were always strong all the way down. We played in the intercollegiates 23 years and we won the doubles more than half the time: 1955-56-

58-61-62-63-64-67-68-69-75-77. We had very good kids who learned so quickly.

For instance, Smith and Lutz were Nos. 1 and 2 in the country in singles as juniors. In doubles they played another team, Bob Hewitt of South Africa and Roy Emerson of Australia, several times in juniors and never beat them. The two teams played in the Pacific Southwest final in 1967 and finally Smith and Lutz managed to win a set (17-15). About four months later, they had improved to the point that they won the national men's indoor doubles.

Smith played the deuce court and Lutz always played the backhand. I mainly worked on their volleys. I taught them to run to the net as fast as they could, but the last step has got to be a long one. For a forehand volley, your left foot is forward. The opposite for a backhand volley. I taught that the forward foot should hit the ground as you hit the ball. That got them inside the service line. I said, "Don't do anything with that first volley unless you have an absolute setup. Just get it back down to their feet. If they get it back, hit it back to their feet again. That might sound difficult, but in doubles it's easy. You only have to cover half the court."

> *Stan Smith:* Bob and I worked together well because he was so solid returning and volleying, and I was aggressive and took advantage of his consistency. He also made some great reflex volleys after I hit bad returns and the opponents ripped it at him. I normally played the forehand side, but one year in the pros we switched and got to the final of the U.S. Open.
>
> George had a great feel for doubles and how to take advantage of his players' strengths. I don't think he recruited for doubles, but he certainly

got the most out of his teams. We all learned some good fundamentals and volleyed well. He taught the serve and volley well and also poaching and movement around the net. I practiced my volley for hours with him.

He worked on getting me more relaxed with my forehand and also had me work extra hard on getting down to the low balls. He saw me play my whole high school senior year and half the freshman year before he made a suggestion to change my forehand. He thought that I would figure it out myself, but I didn't. He had me use a little more wrist to time the ball better and to get more feel control and power. It was interesting that he waited so long. Many coaches will see you play and immediately suggest fairly major changes. It has affected my coaching in that I am not quick to suggest certain changes. I have seen too many different styles that are quite effective. He helped me think about what I might suggest before talking.

We won the school's eighth NCAA men's tennis title in 1967 at horribly hot Carbondale, Illinois, even though some brilliant strategy on my part backfired. When we made the draw, I was hoping that Smith and UCLA All-America Gary Rose would be in the same half, because Stan had beaten him nine straight times. (At the Ojai tournament, I had had Stan play every ball to Rose's forehand and it had broken him down.) I manipulated it by shutting up and letting UCLA get one of its men seeded ahead of my No. 2, Lutz. You put your first and second men in opposite halves. That meant that Rose would play Smith, and I was licking my chops. They met in the quarters and guess what happened. Rose beat Smith 6-4, 6-4. Perhaps by then, Rose was mentally prepared for our tactic of hitting to his forehand incessantly.

We finished the quarterfinals of singles with that match. Then we started the doubles and everything was tight as hell. We were locked up with the Bruins, whereas before we had the edge. With Smith out of the singles, it was really close.

In doubles, two teams from each school were left in the quarters. All four matches were close and all four Trojan and Bruin teams won. Rose lost in the singles semis to Jaime Fillol of Chile and Miami. Both of USC's doubles teams won their semis and Lutz beat Fillol in the singles final and, bingo, it was so close going into the quarters and the next day the Bruins were out.

Lutz's final was unusual. He won the first 15 games and led 6-0, 6-0, 3-0. All of a sudden, Fillol got kind of loose. Smith's recollection is that Fillol had hurt his knee the day before playing soccer with his girlfriend. That year the coaches could sit on the court, and I was trying to keep Lutz from being distracted. Fillol rallied to win the third set. Maybe the heat had helped his knee. Then there was an intermission. Lutz fell behind 4-1 in the fourth set and I had him throw it.

I said, "Bob, I'll tell you what I want you to do. I want you to throw this set. But I want you to do it this way: hit out on every ball. Don't worry about losing the set, but try to keep the point going as long as you can so you can hit a lot of balls that way." I didn't want him to hit eight or 10 balls and the set's over.

He didn't say, as you might have expected, "Coach, you're crazy, I can still win this set." He did exactly as I told him. He just relaxed a little bit and hit out. The fifth set started and he was back in rhythm and won it 6-2.

> *Dan Magill* (ex-Georgia coach): First player to win NCAA singles with a metal racket was Bob Lutz,

Southern Cal, in 1967. He used the Spalding Smasher and this racket is on display at the Collegiate Tennis Hall of Fame, as is the Wilson T-2000 used by Joaquin Loyo-Mayo, Southern Cal, in 1969, and Jimmy Connors of UCLA in 1971.

In the NCAA singles final the next year, at San Antonio, Smith and Lutz faced each other in the final. Stan won 3-6, 6-0, 6-2.

*Stan Smith:* George just watched and didn't say much, except after I lost the first set he came by the back of the fence and suggested that I might stay back a little bit because Bob was killing me with his return. It worked and turned the match around. Later we won the doubles.

During that tournament, George blew up at me, the only time ever. I had just squeaked by Tom Gorman in the quarters and he started yelling about my dogging it and moving badly. He asked if I had been staying out late with this girl I had met. It went on for about 10 minutes nonstop. Finally, I had the chance to explain to him that I had been treated for a sore shoulder and some blisters before the match and then was late, so I ran down the stairs in a hurry and strained my ankle.

He said, "Why didn't you tell me?" I said, "You wouldn't let me. You were yelling so much."

Our Mexican connection kept paying off. In 1969, Joaquin Loyo-Mayo won the NCAA singles title, our third in a row and our eighth in 14 seasons. He and countryman Marcello Lara won the NCAA doubles, the 15th time for a duo from our school. Loyo-Mayo was a little guy, about 5-foot-3, 5-foot-4, so opponents lobbed him a lot. But it didn't bother him. He was very quick. He ran so fast in our training sessions that we would give him a head start and he would run backwards. He could just move like lightning backwards. And he had anticipation. He got lobbed so much in his lifetime that he could just read it right away.

Although he didn't win an NCAA title, Raul Ramirez from Baja California (and La Jolla High School in San Diego) was a force for us in 1972 and 1973. He probably would have been a collegiate champion as a junior or senior, but he turned pro after his sophomore year, with my blessing. I told him, in fact, that I didn't think he should stay in school, because he was not attending class and showed no interest. I knew that he wanted to turn pro, so I advised him. I said, "Raul, you're wasting your time in school."

Raul was ready. He turned pro in June and a few months later when he came to the L.A. Tennis Club for the Pacific Southwest, he had already won a pile of money. And he beat about three or four of the top players in the world. After a fine pro season in 1974, Raul got this compliment from Smith: "I remember him now. He was that 15-year-old George Toley asked me to practice with five years ago. I should have seen him coming."

(John Andrews took over as No. 1 after Raul departed. He was an A student, a first-team All-America in 1973 and 1974 and became a loyal booster of the men's tennis team after graduation.)

> *Sashi Menon:* We were at Notre Dame in 1971 playing in the NCAA's. We were at a restaurant one night and all of us ordered pie. Raul's English at the time wasn't the best, or he had trouble understanding certain words. The waitress came and she rattled off all the pies. And one of them was Boston cream pie. But Raul heard it as bastard cream pie. So he ordered a slice of bastard cream pie.

We were just dying with laughter. George was laughing so hard he got cramps in his cheeks. He was trying to get the cramps out of his cheeks, which only made the rest of us laugh harder.

A little later, Butch Walts, a big kid with a dynamite forehand, and Bruce Manson turned pro early. I tried to talk them out of it but couldn't. Manson definitely wasn't ready.

Jimmy Connors left UCLA after one season. Ditto John McEnroe at Stanford and Erik van Dillen at USC. "We're losing a few players now," I said in 1974, "and will continue to do so, but at the same time, the money offered by tennis in general and the publicity it's getting are strengthening the college game. Many more people are participating than in the past, so the availability to us of more experienced, better-conditioned athletes has increased."

At times, the NCAA has disallowed coaching during a match. I've always been against that. It's a big mistake not to coach during changeovers, because you can tell a player something after a match is over that he should have done and it just doesn't have the same effect. He won't be sure it would have worked. But if he's in a match and losing for a certain reason and you tell him about it, all of a sudden the match completely changes – if you're correct.

James Hobson was playing a tall kid from Trinity, about 6-foot-5, and the guy had a great backhand. So I instructed Jim to serve to his forehand all the time. Jim won the first set about 6-2 and I had to go watch another match. I came back and then he was down 4-1 in the second set. He was missing his first serve and giving his opponent a chance to run around and hit his backhand.

I said, "Jim, don't serve any more first serves. Serve all second balls, and all to his forehand. He's not going to run around it when you serve that first ball. And if he runs around it occasionally, just pound one first serve in there to keep him from doing it."

It makes a tremendous difference in the match when you take away an opponent's cream shot. That hurts them mentally and in every other way.

On most teams, your 1 and 2 players are your first doubles team, and that was the case with Bruce Manson and Butch Walts in 1975. Also, any big weapon, you want in the ad court, be it a forehand or backhand. One of the toughest things in doubles is to win the ad point in your favor. It's easy when it's against you, and many players can win those. You get the ad and often nothing happens.

Now, Manson was a left-hander and always played the ad court. Walts was a right-hander with a great big forehand and he always played the deuce court. Their record was terrible early in the season. They had all sorts of frustrations and wanted to quit. I wanted Walts in the ad court because he had that big forehand and I found he would wail away on ad points and wouldn't miss. So I asked them if they would change and, of course, they looked at me as if I had just lost my mind.

I switched them anyway. In the deuce court, I had Manson just chip his backhand when receiving serve, and then move in. He had a good chip and it worked out well. The combination was a dream and they just sailed through the NCAA Tournament, winning every match in three consecutive sets. It was USC's 16th doubles title.

*Sashi Menon:* George was a master teacher of

doubles. One thing he taught me I used in Davis Cup a number of times. He said, "In doubles, if you get an overhead on an important point, don't try to knock it of – hit it at an angle. Instead, hit it down the middle as hard as you can. You've got plenty of room for error and you'd be surprised how many more points you win." A simple little thing like that – you miss less and the other guys are always looking for you to hit to one corner or the other.

My 10th and last NCAA championship came in 1976 – a tie with UCLA. I had coached teams that were not favored to win the title but never one that was such a heavy underdog as our 1976 squad. It was the most inexperienced team I ever took to the NCAA Championships, too (Walts had left college early). Only Manson had ever played in the tournament, but we scored 21 points to tie the No. 1-rated Bruins, with No. 2-rated Stanford a point behind.

Manson deserved most of the credit for the win. He scored six points in singles by reaching the semifinals, where he lost to top-seeded Peter Fleming of UCLA in a five-setter decided by a tiebreaker. He scored five points with Chris Lewis in doubles, clinching the tie for the title by beating BYU in the semis. Bruce was much more effective than Chris in our doubles wins because Lewis wasn't feeling well.

With few exceptions, tennis until relatively recently has been dominated by whites. Althea Gibson was a pioneering black champion, as was Arthur Ashe at UCLA. USC has had many outstanding African-American athletes, including its first football All-America, Brice Taylor back in 1925. But not many blacks had the opportunity to get into the so-called country-club sports: swimming, golf and tennis. Few, if any, of the top pool of juniors from which I recruited were black.

The best black player I had was Earl Prince, from Hamilton High School in West Los Angeles. He was good, very quick — he won some challenge matches and was No. 1 on the team in 1977, but a strange thing happened with him. We went to Palm Springs and I saw him playing in a match, laughing and not taking it seriously. He was just joking around, he wasn't trying.

Evidently, someone in his religion — I don't recall what religion it was — had convinced him it was not right to be a competitor. I couldn't get him straightened out and he quit school. He didn't play tennis after that. I never saw him on a tennis court.

At about the same time we had Stan Franker, a left-handed native of Surinam (a small former Dutch colony in South America) who played No. 6 for us. He was the 1974 NAIA singles champion for Texas Southern but wanted to transfer to a bigger school. A friend of his brought him to SC and I watched him play and he got a scholarship.

He was a good player at USC, but what he did afterward was far more important. Ashe said Stan was "a gifted minority coach who had to leave the U.S. to become fully employed," and that was true. He left for Europe in 1981, became national coach for the Austrian Tennis Federation and then a big wheel for the Royal Dutch Lawn Association.

Stan gave credit to his social psychology classes at USC, but he didn't feel completely accepted at our school and I feel bad about that. He told Tennis magazine:

"I wanted to use sports to integrate people, because they say sport integrates. But it's not true. On the sports field, guys socialize, but the moment they leave the field, it's over. I saw it at USC. It was a shock to me. You walk into the cafeteria and you have one section that's black and one section that's white. I never saw anything like that in Holland. And in Surinam, the white population mixes with the black population in the clubs. But I have to say that if tennis players were in the cafeteria or a restaurant, I always sat with them and that was never a problem."

*Katie Dempster:* Tennis is a very socially elitist sport, let's face it. For years, only the rich played tennis. Public courts and parks were denigrated and frowned upon. And most of the old, amateur tournaments – and the pro tournaments, when they began – were upper class, with young people whose parents spent the money and joined the clubs and got them the training, got them into the good schools. ... Next to golf, tennis is the sport of business people and the upper class.

That never mattered to my father. He taught tennis on some private courts in Los Angeles to some of the biggest stars in Hollywood and some of the most powerful people in the city. He could do that or he could teach some poor little kid at SC. It didn't matter to him. What mattered was if you wanted to play tennis and you wanted to learn, and you would do what he asked and see if you had the ability to go along with it. That is what mattered.

It didn't matter if you were rich or poor, black, white or any other color. Didn't matter if you were male or female, as long as you could play tennis. That's what he was interested in.

I had so many world-class athletes, from California and elsewhere, that made me and the school look good, that sometimes it's easy to forget the ones who got away. As with Ray Moore of South Africa, USC didn't get every great prospect, not by any means, and sometimes when top kids came, they didn't stay for one reason or another.

Earl Baumgardner was a tall kid from up in the Bay Area with a big serve, and he was a real good doubles player, but there was a peculiar thing about him. In doubles his ground strokes were great, he hardly missed a ball, but in singles his ground strokes weren't that steady. I kept watching and I couldn't figure out what made the difference. Finally I realized what he was doing. In doubles, all he did was hit the ball right at the people at net and that gave him a target. He didn't try to hit down the middle or down the side, he'd just hit at one or other of the opponents, and he could play steady that way. He won the national men's hard courts (with USC alum Hugh Stewart) as a freshman in 1955.

What happened to him, he came to me one day and said he was going to get married. This was about the middle of his freshman year. I said, "What's cooking?" "My future bride is a cashier in a market," he said. "But I'll continue college. We've all agreed. We've talked about it and everything seems fine." I said, "Earl, just a minute. You think she's going to be working in that market and you're going to be sending her letters from Ojai and various places around the country? It's just not going to work."

But he didn't listen and soon left school. The last I heard, he got a pro job, but I don't remember where it was. I haven't heard from him in years.

> *Ed Atkinson:* Baumgardner had a talent that comes along rarely. He was like Ellsworth Vines – just smoked everything. First serve, second serve – he just leaned on it. He was confident and could do anything.

He and I were supposed to play at the L.A. Tennis Club one day. When I showed up, he said, "Ed, do you mind if we don't play today? Gonzalez asked me to play and I've never played him." So I played someone elsewhere and in the junior locker room, he came in and I said, "By the way, how'd you do with Pancho?" "Four and four," he said. "That's pretty good," I said.

I went to the fountain and I was sitting there and Gonzalez is having a Coke and smoking a cigarette. I said, "Pancho, what do you think of Earl? Think he's a pretty good player?" He said, "Yeah, he beat me four and four." Baumgardner! He had said, "Four and four" as I if I should have known who won.

Baumgardner had won the U.S. boys' 18 doubles in 1954 (with Gerald Moss). Then the next year, the event was won by two of my recruits, Greg Grant and a kid from the Philippines, Juan Jose.

Jose enrolled in school and about 10 days later he went back to the Philippines. He had enrolled in engineering and it just overwhelmed him, so he took off.

Making players go to class and pay attention to their studies is frequently a burden for coaches. A guy like Alex Olmedo, if all of a sudden he's ineligible, there goes your season – not to mention the consequences for the man's education.

Circa 1960 we had a fellow who came to school with about a 3.8 grade-point average in high school, so I figured here was a kid I wasn't going to have to worry about. He flunked out his freshman year!

He left USC and went to a junior college, and his father was so mad he made him work at the same time. He made his grades in JC and came back. Toward the end of that semester, when we were getting ready to go to the intercollegiates, Dr. Ed Barker called me and said the man had not attended his class at all. He said, "What do you want me to do?"

"Flunk him," I said.

"George, that's going to hurt the team," Barker said.

"Flunk him," I said again.

I was just so angry that the player would do that to Barker, a fabulous guy who once tutored Osuna for six hours. He was in the school of business and 90 percent of my guys were business majors. The player went into the Army, got out, and according to Dick Leach, earned his degree from Cal State L.A. He got a club job in the South, and he's been there ever since, doing fine as far as I know.

There was a pretty good player from South Africa, a big kid. It turned out that after he was in school and was attending classes, we found out that he had attended some sort of junior college he hadn't told us about. He falsified his entrance exam and his admittance papers, so he was booted out. And we had Eduardo Guzman from Mexico, who was our third or fourth man and played in the intercollegiates for us in the late 1950s. He got homesick after playing one season. His relatives were in business and he had a choice of going into the cement business in Mexico, so he chose to do that. I wish he had stayed a few seasons playing on California cement.

> *Chris Lewis* (USC letterman 1975-76-77-78): I think the biggest lesson I learned from coach is that in life you want to be a complete person. It's not just about winning this match, it's really about how you treat others, how you are respected by others. I

think that's the biggest impact he had on me.

I saw other coaches – all they cared about was win our match, win the NCAA's this year. "I don't care if you go to school. I don't care what happens the rest of your life. It's important to win the NCAA's."

When you're a coach, especially of men that age, you have a tremendous impact. It's obviously a great accomplishment to make somebody a great player, but I think it's a different, more important accomplishment to make him a great person. Or at least a better person. I think that's what George did with a lot of his players. I know he had that impact on me.

I was not usually a yelling, screaming, cursing coach. With a guy like Stan Smith, or Denny Ralston, or Rafael Osuna, it wasn't necessary. But some kids, you had to wake them up. For instance, at times I would have to lay down the law to people who wouldn't go to the net.

Once, Raul Ramirez was playing Sandy Mayer of Stanford in a match at USC, and Sandy was beating him. Raul wasn't punching his volleys. And Sandy was great at running down ground strokes and then passing. Raul was being safe. He wouldn't gamble because he moved so well. He always depended on that, but this was one person it wasn't working against.

After the first set — we could talk on the court then — I just screamed at him, "God damn it, I'm tired of talking to you. Either you're going to do this or I'm going to default you! Make up your mind you can do it!" I cussed him out good. So he went out there and beat Mayer for the first time.

I passed out praise when it was deserved, but I was a bit of a perfectionist, almost always finding some aspect that could be improved. After Manson and Walts had won their semifinal doubles match at the NCAA Tournament in Corpus Christi (they won the final the next day), a fellow coach riding with us was amused to hear the following exchange:

"Coach, do you remember that one shot I made in the second set?" asked Manson.

"How could I forget it," I replied. "It's the only good doubles point you played in the whole match."

> *Ed Atkinson:* He had certain commandments. One was, if you lob over your opponent's head, you must go to the net. You must. You've got to do it. Another was, if somebody hits a short ball and you're coming in, you've got to hit down the line. Never hit an approach shot crosscourt. The reason for that is, if you're hitting crosscourt, you're trying to get to coverage and you're leaving coverage. You're nowhere, you're in limbo. Go down the line and you've got the line locked.
>
> He told me that when I was very young, so I knew it and obeyed. He would lecture the new guys on those cardinal rules. You can't break them.
>
> So now, a new guy drives from school to the L.A. Tennis Club, gets dressed, does some duck walks, warms up. He's in the backcourt and lobs over his opponent's head but stays back. Toley walks on the court and says, "That'll be it for the day. Go take a shower."
>
> The kid wants to play so bad, he couldn't wait to get out and play. And he has to go to the showers. He says to himself, "As long as I live, I'll never do that again."
>
> *Sashi Menon:* The USC men were in Mexico playing

against the Mexicans – John Andrews and I in doubles. All of a sudden George decided he wanted us to lob. He said, "Lob every ball." I said, "Coach, what do you mean?" He said, " I don't care what the situation is, lob every ball". So we lobbed for a game or two. We couldn't understand the thought processes behind this. Maybe it was because of the altitude of Mexico City and we weren't having much success against this Mexican team. Maybe he wanted to break down the rhythm of the other guys.

I remember one particular point, John decided to take a crack at it and didn't lob. George went nuts. He raised his voice and said, "Did I not tell you to lob every ball? What did you just do? Do that once more and you're going back to California."

Sure enough, we kept lobbing.

*James Agate* (USC letterman 1980-81-82-83): Playing for Toley was like playing for Tom Landry on the Dallas Cowboys. Not only did he command the respect that he earned for winning all those championships, but he also earned your respect every day with his actions. He was the best.

One day he put me into play in the singles lineup. As the match started, I was getting creamed by this guy who had a bazooka for a forehand. The score was 3-0, I was setting on the court bench wondering what the hell I should do to at least extend my time on the court when I looked up and Toley was right next to me.

He said, "Jimmy, I don't want to see this guy hit another forehand all day. I don't care what the match score is or where he is located on the court, I want you to hit every single ball to his left side."

So I did for a while. Then late in the first set, I finally hit an approach shot down the line to his forehand. There was no way he could get to hit, but he did, and he hit an amazing shot to pass me.

Coach could be stubborn and he always had a wry sense of humor about it. He looked at me and said, "You're not as smart as I thought you were."

The glare, the chewout, the yell — those are coaching tools I used sparingly. I had one guy who was tearing up all my shirts. When he was losing a point, he'd yank at his shirt, eventually tearing it. We had Lacoste shirts and it was getting expensive. I told him he would have to pay for the shirts from then on. That cured him.

*Jim Buck*: He knew what he wanted and you knew what he wanted and there wasn't a lot of argument about it. One year, we were up at Ricky's, the hotel in Palo Alto. A typical thing for us in the evening was come back from dinner and get a card game going. George would be there playing with us. Everybody probably would have a beer or so. But at 10:30, that was it. Lights out.

One night, Gordon Davis and somebody else decided they'd go to the bar. George walked in, looked at them, didn't say anything. They turned around and out they went. He had certain rules and we didn't bother to question them.

*Dick Leach:* I had a wonderful time at SC and George made it fun for us. We used to play poker, and coach thought he was better than us. Two of the guys I played with, Greg Grant and Bobby Delgado, we went up for the Cal-Stanford weekend and on the return flight we sat in back and played poker. I said, "We're going to use the joker, aren't we?" And coach said, "No." So we took a vote and three of us voted for it. I started getting the joker every time.

Anyway, I took all of George's money. We got to LAX early. He wanted to call Miriam and he reached in his pocket and there wasn't anything there. He had to borrow phone money from me.

He was such a class person and so well respected by everybody. He was just a good example, a pillar of the tennis community. I looked up to George so much and still do today. I've never heard anybody say anything bad about him, ever, and he was honest and straight-up and he would never let us pull any bullshit.

One of the guys on our team once was making some bad line calls, and we went to George and told him it was embarrassing us. He immediately went to that person and said, "You call any ball within a foot of the line good the rest of the year."

*Sashi Menon*: How you behaved on the court was very important to him. He did not tolerate cheating. A lot of other coaches would condone that sort of behavior: If it's close, you call it for yourself. George was just the opposite: if it's close, or if you aren't sure, call it for your opponent. It was a training in life, and his whole approach was like that. He was a classy guy – the way he dressed – in all aspects.

I remember in my senior year I tried to grow some sort of scraggly beard, and that was not a thing he liked. He never said much, but I realized all of a sudden the Ojai trip came and I wasn't on the list to go. I wondered why, because I was one of the better players. I learned very quickly that I better go shave. And I went to Ojai. For him, the image of the team and how the players conducted themselves meant a lot.

One night in 2003 I had to get duded up in a tuxedo and go downtown to the Biltmore Hotel, but the hassle was worth it. Along with my student and coaching successor Dick Leach, I was inducted into the USC Athletic Hall of Fame. We thus joined previous tennis inductees Stan Smith, Alex Olmedo and Dennis Ralston, who had played for me, plus Rick Leach (Dick's son) and Gene Mako. (Bob Lutz got in two years later, and Rafael Osuna went in posthumously in 2007.)

The big banquet room reeked of rah-rah spirit, love and nostalgia, and after I made my way to the dais and accepted my trophy, I made the shortest acceptance speech of the evening:

"It's great to be a Trojan and great to beat UCLA."

## TOLEY'S TIPS — 6

*ASHE AND THE OVERHEAD:* If you can get in position in time, you should hit an overhead pretty much like a serve. One difference between the two is with the overhead the ball is dropping down a little faster because it's coming from a higher height. You should time it to hit it where you would hit your serve, although it's usually a little more in front of you than on the serve. Another difference is that most people don't drop their arm all the way down and come all the way up. They just sling the racket right over their shoulder because it's easier.

Arthur Ashe did something I disagreed with. He brought his racket back and he was waiting, waiting, waiting in that position. He advocated it because the racket was in the ready position, which is true. But there was a loss of fluency, a loss of rhythm, waiting all that time. Ashe didn't generate enough steam his way. If you have your racket back there waiting, you don't have the backward-forward motion that gives you a little more power.

In the same way, a volleyball spiker would lose power if he didn't cock his arm and slash forward with it in an almost-continuous motion.

*PARTNER POSITIONING:* In doubles, if the net player is weaker than his partner, he should stand near the alley to give his partner more shots to play. If the net player is stronger, he should be near the center of the court to (a) give his partner less area to cover, and (b) enable himself to intercept shots directed at his partner.

# ORANGE JUICE, TEA AND TENNIS

Miriam and George Toley
(Photo courtesy of Antonio Novelo, Baja California, Mexico)

# ORANGE JUICE, TEA AND TENNIS

Ojai (pronounced O-hi, with emphasis on the O), is a little town in Ventura County, about two hours drive northwest of L.A. It has been putting on a tennis tournament, known as "The Ojai," for more than a century – a local event but one that has featured the likes of Bill Tilden, Billie Jean King, Pancho Gonzalez, Stan Smith, Pete Sampras, Lindsay Davenport and dozens and dozens of other stars who went on to win Grand Slam titles.

There are umpteen divisions, from little kids on up to all the Pac-10 Conference teams and some local pros. Matches are played all over the county, in public parks, in people's backyards, on hotel, club and school courts, but all the finals are played in Libbey Park in the center of town. At Libbey, freshly squeezed orange juice is served free each morning and free tea and cookies are served each afternoon.

*Chris Lewis:* I played in the 14-and-unders at Ojai when I was in the fifth grade – an 11-year-old playing in the 14s. I lost in about 10 seconds; I think I got a game. I played there from the fifth grade all the way through USC. That would be 12 straight years, and then even after college I played one more year.

I loved going up there, it was so much fun.

I didn't start as young as Chris, but I have been going to The Ojai for about 70 years, since I was a teen-ager. The tournament housed every kid in private homes. Back then the town would close off traffic in the evenings and have dances for the kids on the main drag. (They had an orchestra on a platform. The kids had a great time dancing outdoors at night, until the riffraff from surrounding neighborhoods came and the officials had to cancel it.)

I've played at Ojai, coached there and been just another fan in the stands there. It is one of my favorite times of the year. In 1939, Mel Gallagher and I were runners-up to Gene Mako and Jack Tidball in men's open international doubles. In 1940, Ted Schroeder and I won the intercollegiate doubles for USC, beating a team from UCLA.

*Katie Dempster:* Ojai Valley is a unique place in California. Unfortunately, it is also the hay fever and allergic rhinitis capital of the world, and Dad's hay fever would get out of control. I got that gene and my hay fever would be out of control, too.

So for four or five days, the last week in April every year, we would either have to go to a doctor for cortisone shots or be so heavily medicated we could hardly stand it. But it is a beautiful valley and it hosts one of the best family and all-around tennis tournaments in California and maybe the United States.

We would stay every year at the Ojai Valley Inn. For years in my childhood, from the first grade on, we would go and my parents and I would stay in the same room, with a great view over the golf course. It was off the same hallway that also had the Marlborough girls' team. Girls in high school are fun when they're on a trip. They know how to have pillow fights, how to have slumber parties.

On my father's birthday, April 23, they would have a party for him in the Ojai Valley Inn dining room, which was elegant in those days, and served haute cuisine. The SC team (even if staying in private housing) was always there, the players in dinner jackets, the girls from his Marlborough team dressed up. Generally, they sat at one long table, every other person a college guy, every other person a high school girl. It was fun.

It wasn't just socializing for my Marlborough girls. During my tenure at the school, they won 29 team, singles and doubles titles at Ojai. Penny Winkler in the early 1950s won one doubles and three singles titles.

In 2000, Ojai celebrated its 100th anniversary and brought back many past champions – and many memories. On hand, for instance, was the ambidextrous Beverly Baker Fleitz, who came out of Santa Monica in the 1950s with a left-handed forehand and a right-handed forehand. No need for a backhand. She served right-handed until she hurt her arm; then she served lefty.

She recalled winning the Ojai mixed doubles in 1956 with soon-to-be-husband John. That trip she stayed with an Ojai family who made sure to have cold milk and cookies at her bedside each night.

One evening her hosts gave her permission to go out on a date with John. They returned and were enjoying a goodnight kiss at the door when John's car, the brake improperly set or not set at all, rolled backward into the hosts' swimming pool.

"The good news is that I still got my cold milk and cookies," said Beverly, "but John was not invited back."

That Saturday in April of 2000, Beverly Fleitz presented the trophy to the winning California Interscholastic Federation doubles team from Peninsula High, one of whom was her grandson, Jeff Kazarian.

The stories kept flowing. Pat Henry Yeomans pointed out that her mother, Corinne Henry, won mixed doubles in 1926, Yeomans herself won the mixed in 1939 (with Gene Mako, who was on hand for the 2000 festivities), and Yeomans' son, John, won the men's open singles in 1967.

Jack Kramer remembered that, as a rising star from Montebello High, he won the interscholastic singles at Ojai in 1937 and 1939. He would have won in 1938, too, he said, but he stayed up late the night before a match, losing at poker.

"Kramer lost all our money betting three kings against three aces," said Ted Schroeder. "We had to live off orange juice and cookies from the hospitality tent."

(Oh, the boy Kramer lost to in '38? Arthur Marx, Groucho's son, who went on to lose in the final to Ted Olewine of USC.)

Patty Fendick, women's intercollegiate singles champ at Ojai in 1986 (for Stanford), became head women's coach at the University of Washington.

"My fondest memory is probably the picture board," she said. "We used to laugh at all the old pictures. Now my players come and laugh at the old pictures of me – the bad haircuts and so forth."

Of course, I had to get my two cents in with my favorite Ojai story.

We were wrapped up in a very tight doubles match with UCLA, and John Lesch of the Bruins decided that the officiating was not equal. So he left the court to go to the director of the tournament to try to remove some of the officials.

While he was gone, USC's Pancho Contreras went to the orange juice stand. Now, in those days the court we were on was right next to the orange juice stand. They gave him a pitcher of juice and some paper cups and he went to each linesman and the umpire and gave them a cup of orange juice.

Of course, everybody was just roaring. In fact, I looked over at the UCLA bench and they were also roaring. Because it was tight and everything was so climactic, and all of a sudden this just opened up everything. Everybody thought it was just great.

I don't remember who won the match.

Not so funny was an experience I had in Ojai with future Davis Cup hero Alex Olmedo.

Earlier, we were up at Modesto Junior College and Alex was dogging it. I didn't say much to him. He finally won about 10-8 in the third against somebody he should have beaten 6-1, 6-2. After that match we were going to play Stanford, but it rained and we decided to play the match in Ojai the day before the tournament started.

Alex played Jackie Douglas (who became a huge force in Southern California real estate some years later, as Jon Douglas). Alex had always handled him without much trouble, but this day he lost the first set and was behind 5-1 in the second, because he was dogging it again.

Then, as happened often, he decided he didn't want to lose, and he came back to win the second. But he dogged it again in the third and lost.

So he came over to me and started complaining because our manager didn't have a towel for him. I hit the roof and told him I thought he should get the hell out of my sight, I wanted nothing to do with him. I cussed the heck out of him.

Shortly after that, Eddie Atkinson was playing his match and I happened to look up and there Alex was in the stands, clapping for Ed, and I thought, "Well, I guess he's not going back to Peru. I guess he's staying with us."

At dinner that night – we were at the Ojai Valley Inn – I said, "Alex, right after dinner, I will be out in my car in the parking lot and I want you to come out there." He came out and I sat beside him and said, "I know how tough it is to keep beating people time and time again, but you're getting now to where you're not trying at all."

He said, "I'm having trouble trying."

"You sure look like it," I said. "Now, if you do what I tell you, you'll be OK. Starting tomorrow, no matter who you're playing, I want you to KILL yourself on every ball. Run as hard as you can, run even sometimes when the ball is out. Get physically worn down. I want you to just work your tail off."

He said he would.

The next day, at the scoreboards (it was the regular Ojai tournament now), I looked around and Alex was coming my way. He saw me looking at the scoreboards (it had taken him two long sets to win), so before I could open my mouth, he said, "Coach, wait a minute. I swear I tried. I tried really hard."

"All right, that's all we can ask," I said. "As long as you keep doing that, you're going to be OK."

And he was. He won the singles tournament.

> *Sashi Menon:* The tournament, the orange juice – what a treat. I'd never seen anything like it.
>
> One year at Ojai maybe I was dogging it a little bit. I had to play Bob Kreiss from UCLA in the first round. I remember coach coming to me and saying, "Sashi, you're hopeless. You're not going to win this match." He really got me angry. It was probably the best match I ever played; I beat him 6-2, 6-2, and here's a guy who was like 1 or 2 at UCLA. He didn't get points, I was playing so well.
>
> I walked off the court afterward and I was still fuming. I was so angry at coach that I brushed by him. He grabbed me by the shoulder and said, "It did work, didn't it?" I hadn't understood the simple coaching psychology behind it, but I thanked him later.

As with any of our trips, there were some temptations at Ojai for young men in college.

*Ed Atkinson:* We were at Ojai one year when I was injured. I went anyway because it's such a lot of fun. I lost in the quarters of both singles and doubles. ... We were all staying in private homes, except my teammate Greg Grant was staying at the Ojai Valley Inn. So Bobby Delgado and I and non-Trojan Whitney Reed went to Greg's room to play bridge. We each got a fifth of booze and we were smoking.

About midnight there's a knock on the door. Knock, knock, knock. I said, "Shit, that's got to be Toley." Wiseguy Grant was so sure it was a maid or someone else nonthreatening, he called out, "Toley, if that's you, go ---- yourself." I couldn't stand to ignore the knocking, so I went to the door. It was coach. And there we were with the bottles, the ice, the ashtrays.

He said, "You guys are off the team. And I'm going to do everything I can to kick you out of school." He's pissed at what we were doing and because his players had a bad day on the court.

Jess Hill was the USC athletic director, a straight-laced guy, so we figured we were gone. A few mornings later we were to meet coach at the Tommy Trojan statue and go see Hill. I was saying goodbye to the campus. Toley came up to us and said, "I can't take you to Jess Hill. Not that you don't deserve to, but I know all of your parents and it would break their hearts. I think a lot of them, but I don't think anything of you. But you're off the team."

We get in his car and he talks to us for about an hour about what a tough time he had in school, about how we're screwing up our lives.

We went to the club after that and we played tennis among ourselves. SC was playing teams and getting nailed. On the eve of the match against J.D. Morgan's UCLA team, George came up to us and said, "You guys are playing tomorrow," and walked away. The good news for us was that he hated Morgan more than he hated us.

We went out and we nailed them in a hell of a match.

Two of George's most remarkable traits as a coach were his sensitivity and compassion. And I am living testament to that, because he only suspended me once.

I don't remember the Ojai story quite the way Atkinson does. I never was going to turn them in to Hill. I reminded them of a recent, horrible fraternity hazing incident, in which a pledge choked to death after trying to swallow a piece of raw liver. I said the university was just poised to punish other wrongdoers. We met at Tommy Trojan on Monday, but I said Hill was out of town, come back Tuesday. On Tuesday, I said the athletic director wasn't in, come back Wednesday. And so on. When Friday came, they were haggard looking, three sorrowful characters. They had learned a lesson. And UCLA's legendary basketball coach John Wooden was right when he said he liked to give kids a second chance.

> *Bill Bond:* They used to have these guys up there at Ojai who used to hot rod up and down the street with their lowered cars and wreak havoc with the tennis players. One year I was walking down the street with another player and some of these hoods called us a few names as they drove by. So I

hollered a few things back at them. They stopped their car about 50 yards in front of us. Four guys got out of this Chevy and came toward us. We were each holding two tennis rackets, so we faced them with rackets in each of our hands and I said, "OK, come and get it." They got back in the car and drove away.

We went into Libbey Park and played the match. I walked out through the open area of the park to get to the street and I saw the same car with some other cars and at least 20 guys. I went back inside for help. I got Greg Grant, Ed Atkinson, Jackie Douglas and about half a dozen other college guys who were big as a house. We walked out to the street and it was the darndest thing you've ever seen. Those cars fanned out of there; those guys disappeared in five minutes.

The players came to bat for me, and I was just a 17-year-old kid. That was cool. They could have let me die.

*Sashi Menon:* We used to stay at a ranch, a big spread, outside of Ojai, which George organized for us. The whole team would stay there and it was a lot of fun. One year we were racing down this path and Raul (Ramirez) ran his car into the gates and put a big dent in them. We all got kicked out.

George got very upset, because Raul's remark to this lady was, `Just send me the bill. I'll take care of it." He was flippant about it. Needless to say, we didn't stay there anymore.

"Even people who lost in the first round remember this as one of their favorite tournaments," said famous teaching pro Vic Braden. "I'm still looking for someone who had a lousy time here."

## TOLEY'S TIPS — 7

*THE WORST ERROR IN TENNIS:* It's the double fault, because you're giving a point away before your opponent has a chance to hit long or into the net.

*AMBIDEXTROUS:* Mentioning Beverly Baker Fleitz in this chapter reminded me that I've had people come to learn tennis and they didn't know which hand to use, because they were ambidextrous. I always used the arm they used to throw a ball, because that side would be the most coordinated and strongest, and the one used to serve, which is similar to the throwing motion. A doctor friend of mine had a son who threw with both arms the same way, so I said, ``Pick one side and let me know tomorrow which one you're going to use.''

# WIMBLEDON

Stan Smith
(Photo courtesy of the USC Sports Archives)

# WIMBLEDON

In some respects I felt right at home at the All England Lawn Tennis and Croquet Club, because my home state of California has played such an important part in the club's history and produced so many of its champions. Two women, Billie Jean Moffitt King of Long Beach and Elizabeth "Bunny" Ryan of Santa Monica, won 39 titles between them. The list of champs grows even larger if you count people such as Jimmy Connors, John McEnroe and Rafael Osuna, who went to California universities but grew up elsewhere.

The first overseas winner of any Wimbledon title was May Sutton Bundy. She was the daughter of an English naval captain, but she grew up in Pasadena. Wearing daring short skirts, she won women's singles in 1905 and 1907. Ryan's 19 titles was the record until King came along. It helped that Ryan didn't have to make the long trip by ship; she and her sister moved to England in 1913. All her titles were in doubles. King won her 20th title, doubles with Martina Navratilova, in 1979. Ryan, at age 87, died the day before King supplanted her.

There have been many other champions from California. Helen Wills Moody of Berkeley, wearing her famous white eyeshade, won eight singles titles in the 1920s and 1930s. Maureen Connolly of La Jolla won three in the 1950s before her career was ended by a horseback-riding accident.

The biggest coup in Wimbledon history was, naturally, pulled off in 1939 by Bobby Riggs of Los Angeles. The son of a preacher, he – according to *The New York Times* -- "put together a $500 parlay on himself to win the singles, the doubles and the mixed doubles. It's a large order, but he took the singles on his own, the doubles with Elwood Cooke and the mixed doubles with Alice Marble of San Francisco. The bookies paid him more than $100,000. ..."

The club's raciest scandal featured Santa Monica's Gertrude "Gussie" Moran in 1949. British designer Ted Tinling produced a flattering, sexy dress for her, plus a pair of lace-trimmed panties. The glimpses of the lacy undergarment resulted in photos that were sent all around the world. "I couldn't have caused more of a stir if I had walked out there naked," said Moran.

Anyway, the list of Golden Staters who won on the hallowed grass goes on and on and includes such greats as Smith, Don Budge, J. Edward "Budge" Patty (from my high school in L.A. and USC; he won singles in 1950, doubles in 1957), Ellsworth Vines, Margaret Osborne du Pont, Helen Jacobs, Jack Kramer, ex-Trojan Gene Mako and ex-NCAA champion from USC Bob Falkenburg.

If you include the entire U.S.A., we have done much better on the manicured grass than the English themselves. The Fourth of July comes along during the Wimbledon fortnight. On one Fourth, U.S. players were doing so well that an American reporter in the press section exclaimed, "I'm so proud I feel like standing up and waving my American Express card."

At a press conference that same afternoon, a reporter mentioned to Florida product Chris Evert that Americans were certainly acquitting themselves admirably on the Fourth of July. She said, "Oh, do they have that here?" She thought a second, then joined the laughter at her expense.

Players say they like the French better than Wimbledon. Time and time again they remarked about it. Wimbledon is such a big place and it's kind of stiff. The French are totally different.

For instance – this is just a little thing – when you came to the French and you'd been there before, you didn't have to have a new identification picture made. They just had your old one there and you got it and you were on your way. You got to Wimbledon and you had to have a new picture taken.

The English officials were demanding and they didn't show any kindness or leniency about things. At Wimbledon, there is a whole expanse of courts away from Centre Court. Raul Ramirez was playing at one of them where the stands were full, and his wife could not see the match. She had to sit two courts away and try to peer over hundreds of people to see the action.

I thought I would go to the tournament office, where they doled out balls and stuff, and talk to somebody. Maybe they could get her into one of the boxes that are looking down on the court. So I was waiting at the desk there and I was talking with Rosie Casals and I told her what I was there for.

"Oh," she said, "George, forget it. There's no way in the world that they'll do that here." So I didn't even ask, because she convinced me that I'd be wasting my time. If that had happened at the French, I feel that something would have been done. But that's kind of the atmosphere that you feel when you're at Wimbledon.

Speaking of the outside courts and officialdom at the All England Club, Sports Illustrated photographer Tony Triolo went through some trials in 1974. It was a time when Chris Evert and Jimmy Connors were dating and also playing wonderful tennis— two young American champions in love. Well, Evert won the women's title on the last Saturday, and Connors was favored to win Sunday.

Triolo got the idea that it would make a terrific SI cover photo if he could — should Connors win— get the two alone on a distant court and pose them hoisting their trophies. Wimbledon officials stubbornly nixed the idea of getting Evert's trophy out of the vault. Triolo begged and pleaded and finagled and somehow finally got it approved. And got Evert and Connors to cooperate. In Connors' case, an incident earlier in the tournament probably helped. At one of his matches, his mother, Gloria, had forgotten her Catholic worry beads and was panicked. It so happened that Triolo, from the photographers' area on that court, noted her distress, found out the reason and lent her the beads he always carried with him.

After all the arranging and that hassle with the conservative Brits, Triolo got the pair out on the far court after Connors' victory, but a batch of other photographers got wind of the deal and, benefiting from Tony's hard work, took the same picture for their newspapers. However, his color photo of the beaming pair made the magazine's cover. The lovebird doubles is one of the best tennis covers SI has ever had.

In 1975, when I was 59, a bunch of my former players got together and raised the money to send me and Miriam to our first Wimbledon. But I wouldn't take it for her; I paid her expenses. That was the year Arthur Ashe beat Jimmy Connors in the men's final — damn, I traveled all that way and two Bruins dominated Centre Court — and King won women's singles easily over Evonne Goolagong Cawley.

Seeing my old players in action on the grass was great. I was sitting with my friend and the co-author of this book, Joe Jares, then of *Sports Illustrated*, at Court No. 1, adjacent to Centre Court, to watch Ramirez against Italian Davis Cupper Adriano Panatta on a lovely English afternoon. Bud Collins of the *Boston Globe* and Mike Lupica, then reporting for the *Washington Star*, joined us, sensing a interesting sidebar on an old coach. Lupica wrote this for the *Star*:

"... Ramirez had won the first set, 6-4, but now he was down 2-5 to Panatta in the second, and playing like Zorro without a sword. Ramirez looked up during the change of courts at 2-5, and he saw Toley. Before you could hum a few bars of the Trojan fight song, the new hero of Mexican tennis won the last five games of that set, and was on his way to a straight set victory. 'If I played badly in front of him,' said Ramirez, putting a lot of emphasis on the last word, 'I was afraid he'd have me out on one of the outside courts until nightfall, practicing all the things I had done wrong.' Ramirez was asked what words of praise his old coach had for him after his impressive victory. 'He told me I should have attacked his backhand more,' Ramirez said."

Collins' feature in the *Globe* also went out to other papers. He wrote: "George Toley had been hearing about Wimbledon for years from the disciples he sent across the sea. From the cement courts of Southern California Toley had wandered to the lime lawns presided over by umpires with soft voices and surrounded by roses and hydrangeas. `It's beautiful, everything as advertised,' he said."

And it was. And is.

## TOLEY'S TIPS — 8

*DON'T COME ON TOO STRONG:* Never use all your strength on the serve – 80 percent of your strength is the limit. Remember that power comes from wrist action, and that is increased if at the start the racket is held loosely and tightened just enough to hold on to the weapon before the ball is struck.

*RETURNING FIRST SERVES:* The safest return of first serves is blocking the ball with underspin, with medium speed or slower, at the server's feet if he comes to the net. If the server stays back, the returner should block the ball with underspin to within three feet of the server's baseline.

*DEFENSIVE PLAY FROM THE BASELINE:* Steadiness and depth are the watchwords, and clearing the net high enough is a must for both – three feet to six feet depending on the skill level of the player.

# THE MEXICO CONNECTION

Raul Ramirez
(Photo courtesy of the USC Sports Archives)

# THE MEXICO CONNECTION

Miriam and I often spent vacations down in Ensenada, Baja California. We'd been going there for at least half a dozen years, but I didn't even know there was a tennis court in town. I never even took tennis shoes. We were just on a holiday.

We used to see a tiny sign in those days: "Estero Beach," pointing toward the ocean, six miles. On a trip in the early 1960s, I believe it was, I decided we should take a look at it, and we were surprised to see that it was by far the best place to stay around Ensenada. So we hired a house there for a week.

Estero is less than 120 miles down the wild Baja California coast from the huge border town, Tijuana, and six miles south of Ensenada. Across the bay is a twin of Honolulu's Diamond Head, a rocky promontory called Punta Banda. The desolate beaches nearby must be much the same as when the Spaniards arrived about 470 years ago.

One day I was talking to the girl at the front desk. I said, "We have a wonderful boy from Mexico, Rafael Osuna." I didn't know Tony Novelo, whose office was right in back of the counter. (The resort was founded as a fishing camp for tourists by his grandfather, an Ensenada businessman who went to Estero one day in 1939 to buy some shark liver and ended up purchasing the site of the hotel for $400.) Tony came hurrying out to see me. "Osuna, Osuna," he said, "you said Rafael Osuna?" And that was the start of our friendship.

Tony is a handsome, very intelligent person, well educated and athletic. He played many sports. At the time I met him, he was a pitcher in semipro baseball in Mexico and sort of running the team. He was always running things – so capable. He could have been mayor of Ensenada many times. He was president of the Red Cross three times.

He was just starting in tennis and I gave him a lesson that afternoon. He got me shoes and a racket. They had a club with two courts that was in a mountainous area outside of town. From then on, the Novelo family would have us down as their guests anytime I wanted to go. We could come on 30 minutes notice. Eventually they installed a cement court, snuggled up against a little hill on which sits the Novelo home. I gave everybody in the family lessons – six kids, mother and father.

Lupita was the best in the family. In fact, in the late 1980s, she played about third on our USC women's team in singles and No. 1 in doubles. And she was ranked No. 16 in intercollegiate singles. Her brother Marco was sixth man on our team in the early 1980s. The Novelo family came north for every match.

It was through the Novelos that I got to know the Ramirez family. Raul's father, [Raul Sr.], and Tony played together and used to go on hunting trips together. It was two or three years before Tony built a court at his resort, so I would come down and we would go to the club and play doubles – Tony, the elder Ramirez and myself, and we'd find a fourth.

One day when Raul was about 12, his father said, "George, Raul has gone crazy about tennis. We can't keep him off the court." He had had terrible instruction from somebody in Ensenada. So that summer I had him come live at our house in Westwood. He stayed there a month and I worked him eight hours a day. His dad was head of fisheries in Baja and he would always fill our refrigerator with lobsters and all sorts of stuff. Then every time I would go down there, I would work with Raul.

I can remember one year, when he was about 15, I had a day at the L.A. Tennis Club for young kids, and he played doubles with a boy who was about 12. They played the two boys who were 1 and 2 in Southern Cal in the juniors. And Raul beat them with this 12-year-old! He played almost the whole court to do it, naturally.

In doubles, he almost always hit the ball the right way. I always put him in the ad court. The big thing about the ad court is you've got to have somebody there who can play well there when he gets an ad. That's a real big thing. Some people, when they get an ad, think about something new to do. The man who plays that ad court should just do what he's been doing all along. Don't change, don't think. That's what Raul always did.

That summer we would get to the club in the morning and he would work until noon, do anything I told him. He'd spend a few hours working with the ball machine. When lunchtime came, I'd say, "All right, Raul, go in and have your lunch, and after lunch I want you to have a nap, then come out and work in the afternoon." There was a fellow who took care of the grounds and he let Raul nap on his couch. About 12:30 or 1 o'clock after he had lunch, he would come peering around a corner, wanting to practice instead of napping. So I always had to tell him, "Get that nap."

That summer I put him in the first tournament he played in, which was in Orange County, the 15-and-under division. He lost 6-4, 6-4 and I thought he played a great match, considering it was his first tournament and he was in against a tough player, the No. 1 in Southern California.

Just after Christmas, 1974, Stan Smith and his wife Margie joined me in Baja after honeymooning in California, Australia, Bali, Fiji and Hawaii. Two years before he had been the dominant player in the world, but '74 had been a mediocre year by his standards even though he won $139,120 in prize money. He was in the final eight of both of Lamar Hunt's World Championship Tennis singles and doubles for the second straight time. He was a semifinalist at Wimbledon, blowing a match to Ken Rosewall on Centre Court after having what seemed like an insurmountable lead. I think it was the first match he ever lost after having match point.

I saw a match at the '74 U.S. Championships at Forest Hills, Smith struggling against Jaime Fillol of Chile. I had a theory that when Stan lacked confidence, it showed up in his feet and he started to resemble a cigar-store Indian in the nimbleness department. I called out to him from the stands and he started to get up on his toes and be in motion as Fillol served. Later he was throwing the ball up too far in front of his body on his second serve. I called out some advice and he followed it right away – he was always an apt pupil. He won in a fifth-set tiebreaker and maybe my tips from the stands helped. But he was knocked out in the quarterfinals by hard-serving Roscoe Tanner.

"It finally came to a climax whereby he just couldn't play," said Jack Kramer, then head of the Players' Association, in a *Sports Illustrated* article about Smith. "He didn't want to play, in my opinion, and he lost confidence. He lost to a lot of really inferior players, something he hadn't done before.

"I look at this way: 25 years ago, before open tennis came in and even in the days when we were running pro tours, the champions were people who played 13 to maybe 17 events a year. So all of us guys who achieved our records in those years, we really were .900 hitters. I mean, you won nine out of 10 tournaments if you were the best player because you were always rested and keen.

"Since open tennis has come in, Rod Laver has the best record overall, with Stan and John Newcombe close, but they win roughly one out of four tournaments, so they're .250 batters. Now, if a Smith wants to be an .800 hitter, it's possible, but he's got to go back to our philosophy. Play 15 tournaments and play 'em all damned good, or play 25 or 30 and play 10 or 12 bad. That's all."

Besides Smith at Estero that Yule season, there was his Davis Cup doubles partner, Erik van Dillen, and Ramirez, who lived in Ensenada, and Mark Novelo, who was 15 then. I worked the four of them on conditioning, having them run in the sand while I took it easy in a jeep up ahead, ordering the driver to alternately speed up and slow down as they struggled to keep up.

I used a videotape recorder at the practices on the Novelo court, then analyzed their every tic in sessions in my room. I didn't recommend any radical changes in Stan's game. I thought he had been too timid on backhand service returns, waiting to make sure where the ball was going, then making sure to get the ball back. I had him stand closer and got him to start moving almost before the server struck the ball, maybe missing a few more balls but making some outright winners more often or some real tough shots more often.

I also felt Stan had been too cautious getting to the net after serving. He was running to about a step back of the service line, or at most, to the service line, and kind of waiting to see where the ball was going to go, and then moving. I tried to get him to move inside that service line, then he'd still have time to wait. The interval would just be shorter. Then he'd be up there close where if someone did have a weak return, he could simply gobble it up at the height of its arc and do something with it.

We worked on having him gamble more at the net, anticipating instead of always being dead sure, on putting more underslice on volleys for better control, and on serving with a little more explosion instead of a continual rhythm. He had been trying so hard not to miss the ball and not get passed that his movements weren't natural enough.

At the end of that wonderful stay in Estero, Stan told

*Sports Illustrated*, "...I'm really eager to play. It's a lot different story than the last three years."

Well, he never was the world's dominant player again but played five more years of Davis Cup and won eight more national titles in the U.S., Australia and South Africa, including two U.S. Open doubles championships. He struggled with elbow problems off and on from the middle of 1975 to 1977, when he had an operation, and did not threaten to be No. 1 again in singles.

> *Rafael Belmar Osuna* (USC letterman 1986): Coach Toley had his tennis camp in Cuernavaca, Mexico, for the best junior players in the nation. It was 1978 and I was 13 years old. I had known coach for a long time and he always took extra time with me, especially since the year before I had studied in Ireland and my English was very good. We could communicate fluently.
>
> One afternoon he instructed us on the way to hit a deep defensive lob. He did not want us to use a topspin lob since that is a very hard shot to master. ... At that time, players like Vilas and Borg were very popular and hit marvelous topspin lobs.
>
> After a while, while we were on the courts practicing and I had had enough time to forget coach's speech and feeling pretty cool about my personal capabilities, I had the misfortune of him catching me hitting a topspin lob. He stormed onto the court and stood in front of me, a towering figure, and called over the tennis pro assigned to my court. This pro was a friend of mine, 20 years old, and knew me well.
>
> Coach told him, "Translate and repeat after me."

"He understands English," said the pro.

"Do YOU understand English?," said Toley. "Translate and repeat after me."

I was then chewed out so badly that I only remember the last two things coach said: "If there is something that I truly hate, it is stupidity."

And as this giant slowly walked away, he said, "And regarding me having a translator present, I thought you would understand better if you heard it this time in *stereo*."

I operated those camps, in Cuernavaca and other cities, for five or six years. My compensation? Not a peso, but instead free rent at the Novelos' resort and a great head start in recruiting Mexican players for USC.

Pancho Contreras, my first recruit from Mexico at USC, has a great sense of humor and a lively imagination. He was on the road as a touring pro nine to 10 months a year from 1957 until 1965. A crazy life, a crazy schedule. For instance, he played Davis Cup against Canada on grass and the following Monday had to play on clay in Toronto, losing 6-1, 6-1. The flights from Mexico to Australia took 52 hours in those days. He wasn't at home in Mexico for the birth of any of his kids ("Lucky they look like me," he says.)

So he and his wife Maria named the children after wherever he was in the world at the time of their births: Francisco Wimbledon Contreras, Javier Altamira Contreras, Maria de Lourdes Contreras and Rachel Brisbane Contreras.

When Pancho turned 66 and had been playing 55 years, he invited a mob of friends and relatives to an indoor tennis club. The first point was against his wife, the last against son Javier, an ex-Mexico Davis Cupper. He played 120 points vs. 120 different people. He gave a shirt with a special logo to everybody who participated. It took four hours, 54 minutes and the ball went over the net 2,425 times.

Pancho had several careers in Mexico – sportscaster for big tennis matches in Mexico City, disc jockey, vice president of sales for Eastern Airlines' Mexico and Central America divisions, marketing director for Coca-Cola down there. He was also the country's table tennis champ. He traveled a long way from a troubled boyhood — he had no mother or father from the time he was 12. He and four brothers lived with an uncle and aunt. His father, a dentist, was a track & field Olympian in 1924 and 1928; he drowned in the ocean. His mom died at age 34 of a brain tumor. Tennis was his way out, or, as he says, "The racket for me was the solution."

I love Mexico and the Mexican people, and that love has been returned. The greatest tennis audiences I have seen are in Mexico City. At Davis Cup and other events, they were rooting like hell for their players, but they were rooting for the opposition players, too. I've been to that city maybe half a dozen times and I'm telling you, they're as good an audience as you could find.

The crowd was experienced with tennis. The big events were held at Chapultepec Park, at a club with 10,000 members, Centro Deportivo Chapultepec.

A small event, but big for me, came when Estadio George Toley was dedicated at the Novelo family's Las Rosas hotel south of Ensenada. It's a gorgeous place. More than 200 people were there, including the Ramirez family, Rafael Osuna's sister and son, ex-USC players Don Eisenberg, Bill Bond, Stan Smith and Jim Buck. It's a beautiful little stadium right by the ocean. One court with a plaque on the side generously dedicated to me.

*Bill Bond:* All the big shots from Baja were there, particularly from Ensenada. George got to say a couple of words. It was a really major event for Mexico, because not only had George helped the players, but he also had helped create a great history for Mexican tennis players. The Mexicans feel like George had influenced the guys to come to SC and get a good education and actually had paved the way for them to go into the professional tennis world and, indirectly, Davis Cup success.

*Jim Buck:* They invited a bunch of people from SC to come down for the dedication ceremony and afterwards we had a fantastic dinner. There were a lot of speeches in Spanish, then they went back and talked in English and told what was going on. They referred to George as The Father of the Mexican Davis Cup Team. (The honor continues. One of his students, Jorge Lozano, became Captain of the Mexican team in 2008, after the coach had died.)

*Rafael Belmar Osuna:* He is the Father of Mexican Tennis, period, and here are a few of the reasons why. Eighty-six percent of all the Grand Slam champions from Mexico were his pupils. Five of Mexico's Davis Cup captains were his pupils: Francisco Contreras, Eduardo Guzman, Yves Lemaitre, Eduardo Martinez Lanz and Raul Ramirez. Five of Mexico's Federation Cup captains learned from him: Elena Osuna, Alejandra Vallejo, Claudia Hernandez, Raul Ramirez and Joaquin Loyo Mayo. The Mexican Federation Cup team that advanced the farthest was led by three of his students, the captain and two of the players.

Mr. Toley served as the honorary chairman of the board of directors of the nonprofit organization Rafael Osuna Sports Foundation, A.C.

The Osuna Foundation helps handicapped athletes train and compete in national and international events, and it helps connect Mexican athletes with foreign universities, mainly in the U.S. One of the best players to receive such assistance was Daniel Langre, who played on USC's 2002 NCAA-championship team.

## TOLEY'S TIPS — 9

*LOFT OF THE LOB:* The height of the lob shouldn't always be the same. The farther out of position the defender is, the higher the ball must be lobbed. Yes, this gives the opponent more time to get in position to hit an overhead, but it also gives the defender more time to recover and get to the center of possible return.

*ONE MORE BALL:* Sometimes a player gets in a desperate situation during a point and gives up, figuring he or she will get back into the game or set on the next point. That's faulty thinking. The opponent should be made to hit another ball whenever possible. Especially on crucial points, top players have blown easy chances.

# ROAMING THE WORLD WITH RAMIREZ, THEN RETIREMENT

George Toley in an off-court moment
with Raul Ramirez
(Photo courtesy of the USC Sports Archives)

# ROAMING THE WORLD WITH RAMIREZ, THEN RETIREMENT

In 1980, Raul Ramirez was not playing well, and he came back to Los Angeles for a pro tournament at the L.A. Tennis Club. He was going to play Brian Gottfried in the final and Brian had beaten Raul something like seven times in a row. Gottfried was near the top of his game. It was the beginning of the season and he had won two or three tournaments in a row. He was high in the rankings.

Raul and I were in the locker room before the match and I asked him, "What's happened?"

"Well, George, when we get in a baseline rally, he can rally with me," said Raul. "Then he gets that short ball and he uses that undersliced backhand." Brian had a beautiful, biting, undersliced backhand. "He comes in and it's hard to pass him."

What had happened was Raul had become a baseliner. I didn't know it. And he'd always been a volleyer, a great one.

"If you follow it, I'll give you a suggestion," I said. "I want you to go to the net on *every* one of your serves, and I want you to go in there on every one of his serves if you possibly can."

He won the match. The only time he stayed back, against my orders, he lost the second set. Got into a rally with Gottfried, which is the last thing I wanted him to do. *Don't* rally with this guy.

He won mainly because, except in that second set, he never gave Gottfried a chance to get in a groove before he — Raul — went in to volley. The points were ending quickly and Gottfried was the kind of guy who had to get in a groove. Raul went in on everything and, you know what? He won despite volleying terribly, because he hadn't been doing it enough in matches.

The same thing that happened to Gottfried happened to Ivan Lendl in the French Open final against Michael Chang in 1989. Chang hurt himself. If he had not hurt himself, he would have lost. Lendl won the first two sets, then Chang suffered cramps. Lendl felt, "I'll just get the ball back against this guy. He can't run anymore." The Czech lost his rhythm, he lost his aggressiveness and that cost him the match.

Anyway, I think that strategy session convinced Raul that he wanted me to coach him. He and his dad and I had a meeting and he said he wanted me to travel with him and be his coach. His agents wanted him to hire Roy Emerson, the great Australian champion, but he hired me.

I didn't get a percentage of his winnings. I was on a flat rate. We had a contract that was drawn up by one of the leading attorneys in L.A., Ed Hookstratten, an ex-USC baseball player who handled the affairs of many pro athletes and coaches.

A few weeks later, Raul told a reporter for the *L.A. Times* about his change in attitude the year: "Suddenly it hit me. I said to myself, `Raul, what are you doing? You lose in the first round in Rome and the first round in Paris and what do you do? You party and you get lazier. Are you crazy? You are getting ready for Wimbledon two days before it starts? And you don't even know where you're going to practice.'"

Raul had been 7th, 5th, 7th and 8th in the world, he had won the Italian Open in 1975, nearly half a million dollars in 1976 and many doubles titles with partner Brian Gottfried. He had been No. 1 in doubles and ended on top one year in the Grand Prix in doubles and singles. But in 1979 he finished 41st in the world. He was closer to 30 than 20 and he had lost his competitive edge.

It wasn't a tough decision for me to leave USC, because after 26 years on the job, I was going to retire anyway and I wanted to try going on the circuit. To replace me, I called 39-year-old Dick Leach, a third-team All-America for us in 1961 who had played No. 3 his senior year behind Rafael Osuna and Ramsey Earnhart. Leach had done well in building tennis clubs in Big Bear, Westlake Village, Irvine and Ojai.

> *Dick Leach:* I thought he meant the next year. I asked him when I'd be starting and he said, "Next Monday." That was kind of a shock.

He was a fine choice. The team went 22-5 the rest of the way and Robert Van't Hof won the NCAA singles title. Leach stayed for 23 seasons. He was Pac-10 coach of the year five times. His teams won six Pac-10 titles and four NCAA titles, the final one coming at College Station, Texas, in his final season, when the Trojans were only the No. 11 seed.

I started on the circuit with Ramirez in March of 1980. I took care of travel arrangements and I scouted his opponents. I took movies of his opponents, in fact — the first color videos used in coaching the sport. If we had to make a dinner appointment, I would take care of those things. I was a traveling secretary as well as coach.

We got together and figured out the schedule. It was relatively easy then because there weren't that many tournaments. You had to play in the main events, you didn't have a choice in those days. It was always cut and dried. The first year it was just him and me. The second year, we had a little entourage, me and Miriam, Raul and his new wife, Maritza Sayalero from Venezuela, who had become the 28th Miss Universe in 1979.

In November of 1979, Raul's dad had asked him to come home to Baja to attend a reception for the new Miss Universe, a lucky trip for him. She was a beautiful girl, obviously, and a wonderful person. They got married in Ensenada in December 1980.

She got pregnant while we were on the circuit. One morning about 2 o'clock in Italy, she got sick. So Raul and I got dressed and went around looking for a drugstore to get medicine for her.

We didn't do much tourist touring. Miriam and I did a little the second year, but only a little. When you're on the pro tennis tour, first of all you get up in the morning and go out to practice. Then it's almost time to play a match. It keeps you so busy that you don't have time to do much sightseeing. The old USC team camaraderie wasn't much in evidence on the pro circuit. What togetherness existed came mostly from Davis Cup and business interests.

> *Stan Smith:* We started a company, Players Enterprises Inc., including Ashe, Pasarell, Ralston, Riessen, Tom Gorman, Dick Stockton and Roscoe Tanner. Men from USC, UCLA, Northwestern, Seattle, Trinity and Stanford. We invested in different tennis businesses and were friends because of this and Davis Cup. The USC connection did not follow into the pros much.

> Arthur and I always had a bet on the USC-UCLA football games. The basketball was too one-sided (for UCLA) to bet.

Raul would always dine in the best places. Every hotel or big restaurant knew him. There was one place in London where the line to get in was half a block long. We got there and Raul didn't stop at the back of the line. I said, "Raul, where are you going?" He said, "Don't worry." So we got to the door and the manager of the restaurant said, "Oh, Raul, hi!" Two minutes later we had a table.

Money wasn't a big thing with him, he was always loose with it. For instance, he wanted to travel first class on airplanes all the time. I'd say, "Raul, we're going from L.A. to San Francisco and you're paying first class. We sit down, and get up almost before we're finished sitting down, and you're paying first class." Before I joined him, he would only book a flight the week he was playing. That was very costly. Finally I got him to buy tickets for all the tournaments in advance and he saved himself maybe 40-50 percent.

One of my main roles was to keep him aggressive, because he didn't want to make any errors. That was the main thing I kept hounding him about. We worked on his serve a lot and improved it. His accuracy on his serves was always good; it was the velocity that was the problem. He didn't use enough wrist and I got him to use more.

Ramirez had many great opponents out on the tour those two years: Smith, Lutz, Gottfried, Jimmy Connors, John McEnroe, Peter Fleming, Bjorn Borg, Guillermo Vilas, even Hans Gildemeister from Chile and USC. I say "even," because Gildemeister lettered for me in 1974-75-76, on teams with Chris Lewis, Sashi Menon, Butch Walts and Bruce Manson, and was not an All-America. He had talent, but he volleyed with two hands when he arrived and we soon changed that. I left his ground strokes alone.*

> *Hans Gildemeister* in the *Palm Springs Desert Sun*: I knew USC was the best college to go to because Smith, Lutz, van Dillen, Ralston, Osuna, Olmedo — all those guys were coached at USC by Toley. I learned first it was very important for me for lifestyle to go to USC. I was there for three years, met different types of people from all over the world. The most I learned was about tennis. I learned a lot from our coach, George Toley.

Back to Ramirez. Raul was past his best days those two years, but there were some fine moments. In 1980, at the WCT Tournament of Champions, it took the great

---

* His last season was kind of a disaster. He took off the first semester and he came back way out of shape. He spent a lot of time on Fraternity Row while he was at SC. He was a good-time sort of a guy. He sank down to No. 6 on the team and complained about it, until I showed him the challenge-match results.

He turned into an outstanding professional, winning four singles and 25 doubles titles. He was a damn good doubles player. He was ranked No. 1 in the world in doubles at one time.

John McEnroe to knock him out in the fourth round. He made the final in Florence and the doubles final of the French Open. He and Gottfried beat Smith and Lutz in the final at Ponte Vedra Beach, Florida, and got $20,500 each.

At Wimbledon in 1980, he lost in the first round to Shlomo Glickstein after having match point. He lost matches when he had leads like that, which he never used to do. Now when he got those leads, he got tight. He didn't have the confidence he had had when he was at his best.

One of Raul's greatest wins when I was with him came in Milan, Italy, early in '81. He and Gottfried beat McEnroe and Peter Rennert 7-6, 6-3 in the final and won $5,250 each.

Everybody thought McEnroe's backhand was his weak shot, because he had no power on it. But he seldom missed it. And his backhand volley was the same way. When he came to the net to volley on the backhand side, opponents would usually hit down the line to his backhand, and he wouldn't miss the thing. Before this match, I told Raul to hit every ball to McEnroe's forehand and that helped win the doubles for him and Brian.

Later, in Wimbledon singles, Raul beat Ray Moore of South Africa in straight sets, and gave McEnroe a good battle in the second round before losing 6-3, 6-7, 6-3, 7-6. Using the same hit-to-his-forehand strategy, it was a set all and Raul had three set points to go ahead two sets to one. On one set point, he didn't hit his first serve hard, just got it in to McEnroe's forehand. John hit the corner crosscourt.

That's the way Raul was. His competitive ability was not there when he was ahead. That's when he had his problems. He lost many matches after he had match point.

Otherwise in '81, he reached the final of the U.S. Pro Championships in Philadelphia, the final of doubles at Richmond, Virginia, and the singles final at Florence, Italy, the doubles final on clay in Indianapolis. With Pavil Slozil, he won doubles at the U.S. Pro Tennis Championships at Brookline, Massachusetts, and at Washington, D.C.

He did OK in Davis Cup, too, although McEnroe kept getting in his way. Just before I joined Raul, Mexico lost to the U.S. in Mexico City, Raul falling to McEnroe in singles and he and Trojan alumnus Marcelo Lara losing to McEnroe and Peter Fleming in doubles. In March of '81, Mexico lost to the U.S. in Carlsbad, California. Raul beat Roscoe Tanner, and with ex-Trojan Jorge Lozano beat Marty Riessen and Sherwood Stewart in doubles. But McEnroe beat Raul in the deciding, contentious singles match 6-4, 6-3, 6-0.

"I think he complains too much," said Ramirez of his conqueror. "I don't think it's nice. When you're on the court, not too many players like it when the opponent complains. He's a great player, maybe he truly thinks all of his shots are in."

"He's the king of doing that," said McEnroe. "What's he talking about? Everyone has a right to complain. It's hypocritical of him to say that."

The main thing that kept Ramirez from doing even better at the end of his career was his tendency to get injured. Three times in my tours with him, we had to leave the circuit, come home and give him time to recuperate. In the first tournament together, in Frankfurt, Germany, he won this match in the third round. In that tournament, he gutted out a tough 6-

7, 7-6, 7-5 win over John Sadri in a match that lasted nearly four hours. ("A breakthrough," Raul called it. "I showed I could concentrate for a long time and win.") Our hotel was right across the street from the auditorium. We got back there — I think after the Sadri match — and he said, "George, I've pulled something." He had pulled a groin or stomach muscle. The next day he played Stan Smith — he won the first set and then lost the next two because he couldn't serve effectively. So we went home. It was all we could do. And that happened three times. After the second year with Raul, he retired and I decided to do the same.

# TOLEY'S TIPS — 10

*LUCK OF THE DRAW:* Be a positive thinker. When I first traveled Europe with Raul Ramirez, he said, "George, I'm never going to be a Wimbledon champion. I've been doing this for about six years now. I just don't have it to be the No. 1 in the world."

I tried to impress upon him that anything could happen. In 1946 a Frenchman, Yvon Petra, who wasn't all that great won Wimbledon, beating Geoff Brown in the final in five sets. Not long after, Petra came to the Pacific Southwest tournament in Los Angeles and Ted Schroeder routed him. And Chuck McKinley won Wimbledon in 1963, partly because he had the good luck to meet an unseeded player, Fred Stolle, in the final. He beat the Aussie 9-7, 6-1, 6-4.

I have found that often the luckiest players are well prepared (most important) and optimistic.

*SERVING SLOW TO FAST:* Some people's serves are, from beginning to end, a kind of continual rhythm. To get more power, serve with an explosion at the end. Try to gather all the momentum you can with your racket head. It's kind of like a shot putter: He moves across the ring quickly and smoothly, then all of a sudden he explodes to throw the iron ball.

I say, "Slow to fast." Take your time at the beginning of your serve, then at one precise moment, really accelerate as fast as you can. Usually you can hit the ball harder that way.

*RELAX ON THE SERVE:* On no stroke is it more important to be relaxed than on the serve. Thus you cannot have a tight grip on the racket. Either hold it very loosely throughout or very loosely at the beginning and squeeze just enough at contact to be able to hang on to the racket.

Actually, avoid a tight grip all the time, because it tires out a player and prevents the racket from doing its work.

# EPILOGUE

Coach Dick Leach, Goperge Toley's successor
(Photo courtesy of the USC Sports Archives)

# EPILOGUE

For 25 years I had had four jobs. I was always at Marlborough at 8:30 in the morning and worked with the Marlborough girls. Taught them there, went to tournaments with them. At the same time, I was working at SC, teaching at the L.A. Tennis Club and running the tennis shop. So before I retired I often had to do things around the house at 2 o'clock in the morning.

After 1981, I worked around the house and played doubles three, four, five times a week with my pals. I was very comfortable, I enjoyed it.

Except when I was on the road, four of us, Leonard Straus, Joe Davis, Barry Bosley and I, had a regular doubles game for about 30 years. Straus was president of Thrifty Drug and very successful and generous. USC would play a match and he would come up to me and give me $100 or $150 and say, "Take the guys to dinner" He did that often. He also helped build the tennis complex at UCLA. Bosley had a fabulous hair-restoring business — something like 18 shops. Davis was a salesman — stoves was one of the things he sold for years.

All three were well off financially and liked to bet heavily -- $1,200 was the most. I didn't participate in that part of it, but if my side won, I always got a little share of the winnings, so that put on a little pressure. It was always friendly, though.

[Davis was Bobby Riggs' pigeon. Before the matches, they would be in the locker room of the L.A. Tennis Club, hassling for about an hour to decide what the odds would be in the match – what they were going to bet and who played with whom and what the handicap would be. Finally, I got to feeling sorry for him and I said, "Joe, let's try something. Before you've decided, check with me and I'll tell you what I think" Most of the time, I'd say, "Joe, no, don't do it" And he would say, "George, I just got this new handle and it just feels great" I would say, "Fine, but try to get a different bet. The odds are not right for you" (For some years, Riggs didn't play much tennis. He played golf in New York. But when he came to L.A., the day he arrived he would look up Davis and be on the tennis court and betting.]

They were good amateur players. Straus won a lot of veterans' tournaments. Toward the last, I was not much better than they were. I couldn't grouse to myself or anybody else about that, because I had played good tennis for a lot of years. I took pride in being able to hit and sometimes even compete with my USC players.

As you get older you have to change your game; you miss your younger reflexes. But you can still be a good player, and the only way to be good is to keep playing.

*Dick Leach:* When I was on the SC team (1959-60-61), George could still play. My friend Bob Potthast, who had a tremendous serve, would go to the club and play with me against him and Rafael Osuna. And bet lunch on it. And George was able to keep up with us, even though we were all younger. He was 45 or 46 and he could still play.

*Sashi Menon:* He played doubles with us all the time. Just real solid.

*Chris Lewis:* Early in my years at SC, I had hurt my shoulder and I wasn't playing very well, so George took me up to a court somewhere in Beverly Hills and we played. I was beating him pretty badly and I thought, "Boy, I'm getting pretty good now," because George was in his mid- to late-50s, but you had to play well to beat him. He had a good serve and played high-probability tennis.

I remember him playing doubles with us and serving harder than Butch Walts, who was a real strong guy. We were all shaking our heads and asking ourselves, "How is this happening?"

*Ed Atkinson:* George had a high threshold for pain. I remember one time Alex Olmedo was playing him in about 98 degrees. There was no air. Alex gave him three games and the serve for five bucks. Toley thought there was no way Alex could beat him. Coach was about 46.

And Alex beat him. It was worse for Toley because he was doing more running and it was so hot. I was getting tired just watching from the sidelines. Toley said, "Double or nothing" Alex said, "I'll give you four and serve" So it went another 40 minutes and, God, Toley was about to die. So asshole Alex said, "OK, coach, I'll give you five and serve" Toley said, "Serve 'em up"

*Rafael Belmar Osuna*: During the 1985 USC tennis

fundraiser at the LATC, the men's varsity played a doubles tournament with the tennis team patrons, George Toley amongst them. A member of the USC team would partner with a patron and we would play eight-game pro sets.

In order to compete the draw there was a team composed to two USC players, Luke Jensen (who would later win the French Open doubles title with his brother Murphy) and John Washer. I was partnered with Toley. On paper it clearly looked to be a mismatch. I was 22, Jensen was 18 and Washer 21. Toley was 70. I was able to get into my teammates' heads by telling them before the match that I was going to poach on every single one of their returns – which I did successfully. Washer was not a very good doubles player and got tight right away. I guessed he was nervous playing alongside Jensen and not doing well against a 70-year-old. Jensen was getting frustrated with his partner not being able to return Toley's serve in a match that should have been a walk in the park.

Toley's play was amazing, especially considering his age, that the USC guys were not doing him any favors — hitting the ball and trying to win. Luke behaved at all times like a gentleman, not at any time hitting an intimidating shot at coach. After every point I ran and picked up the balls on our side so that coach would be rested. Coach stood his ground, especially at the net, hitting all the volleys deep, exactly the way he taught. We lost the set 8-7. We played a tiebreaker at 7-all in front of a medium-sized crowd of past and present USC tennis players and LATC members. Everybody in the audience was extremely surprised at how well coach Toley played.

I finally had to give up playing because of my back, which first started giving me problems in the 1960s. One morning I woke up and couldn't move. My back was very painful. Really bad. Back then I went to the doctor who treated SC athletes. He thought maybe it had been caused by my serve, because in my prime we used the twist serve — hit the ball in back of our head and turned our body. It was weird. I had never felt pain when I served, perhaps because when I served I always used my wrist, which gave me all the power I needed.

From then on it kept getting worse. I had all kinds of examinations and I had back surgery. There was nothing the surgeon could tell me about the back except there was a little cartilage loose between my vertebrae. He didn't really say that that was my problem, but it was the only thing he found that was worth mentioning. Eventually, tall George Toley was bent over almost in the shape of an L.

On the night of Saturday, June 16, 2007, there was an event in my honor held in the banquet room of the Galen Center, USC's new arena. It was supposed to be a surprise, but my daughter and son-in-law figured that a 91-year-old retiree should be prepared, so they tipped me off just before. Organized by Bruce Manson, Bob Lutz and Chris Lewis, the event had about 200 of my ex-students from USC, the LATC and Marlborough School. There was a contingent there from Mexico, including the Novelo family from Baja California. Stan Smith came in from Hilton Head, Dennis Ralston from Colorado, Manson and Jerry Cromwell from New York City.

There were a lot of nice things said about me. I told the crowd that only about half of it was true, but I appreciated the comments anyway and blessed them all.

*Stan Smith* at the dinner: George has proven he can truly turn hamburger into steak. All you have to do is look at me, or look at Alex Olmedo, or Rafael Osuna. All of us came to USC with really not many credentials, and left USC playing a little bit better. In fact, I bet most of you in the room can vouch for that same thing, that the time you spent with George not only improved your tennis but probably improved your life.

Well, teaching the caliber of people who joined me in the Galen Center that night was almost always a joy. Being involved in the wonderful sport of tennis was almost always a joy. If I had it to over again, I would do it the same way. Everything was on the plus side – the jobs I had and the people I knew. I played tennis all year. It was a pretty hard life to beat.

*Joe Jares*: George Toley died March 1, 2008, at Huntington Memorial Hospital in Pasadena, about two months short of his 92nd birthday. He was admitted February 3 and was about to be released February 11 when, Dr. Eric Lee told me, he took a turn for the worse. Among his problems: a heart attack and an inability to swallow. I visited him on February 22, along with his ex-players Chris Lewis and Bruce Manson, but he was heavily doped up and sleeping. His daughter Katie told us it was just a matter of days, maybe hours. I didn't have a chance to tell him I loved him and that he was one of the finest gentlemen I had ever met in many decades of covering sports.

An announcement from his family said, "His ashes have joined those of his beloved wife, Miriam, at sea. In his honor the University of Southern California has established The George Toley Memorial Tennis Fund, c/o Ron Orr, USC Athletics, Los Angeles, CA 90089-0602."

I'm grateful that he had a chance to read this book in manuscript form, that he was able to enjoy a big celebration of his life staged by his ex-players at USC's Galen Center (June 16, 2007), and that he made it into three halls of fame when he was still alive.

I and others have been trying to get him into the International Tennis Hall of Fame in Newport, Rhode Island, an honor he richly deserves. The Hall has a clothes designer (Ted Tinling), administrators (including Perry T. Jones) and journalists (including Bud Collins), which is fine, but there are no coaches. (Yes, Australia's Harry Hopman was a good coach. George confirmed that for me. But Hopman is in there mainly as a Davis Cup captain for the Aussies.)

Can you imagine a football hall of fame without Knute Rockne of Notre Dame or a baseball hall of fame without John McGraw of the New York Giants?

Think of the words "tennis" and "international" Either one could have been George Toley's middle name. He ought to have a niche in Newport. A group of his admirers are going to keep campaigning for it.

# APPENDIX

# THE TOLEY CHAMPIONSHIP RECORD

**1948**
U.S. Boys' 15 doubles — Allen Cleveland

**1949**
U.S. Public Parks 18 Singles — Allen Cleveland

**1952**
U.S. Hard Court Mixed Doubles — Julie Sampson
U.S. Hardcourt 18 Doubles — Allen Call
U.S. 18 Singles — Julie Sampson

**1953**
Australian Mixed Doubles — Julie Sampson
Australian Doubles — Julie Sampson
Italian Doubles — Julie Sampson
U.S. Hard Court Boys' 18 Doubles — Brooke Grant
U.S. 18 Doubles — Nancy Dwyer

**1954**
U.S. Interscholastic 18 Singles — Gregory Grant
U.S. Chamber of Commerce 15 Doubles — Joe Cowley

**1955**
U.S. Hard Court Doubles — Earl Baumgardner
NCAA Doubles — Francisco Contreras
NCAA Doubles — Joaquin Reyes
NCAA Team Title — USC
U.S. Hard Court 18 Singles — Gregory Grant
U.S. Hard Court 18 Doubles — Edward Atkinson
U.S. 18 Doubles — Gregory Grant
U.S. 15 Doubles — Sally Moore
U.S. Jaycee Singles — Earl Baumgardner
U.S. Jaycee Doubles — Earl Baumgardner

**1956**
U.S. Hard Court Singles — Alex Olmedo
U.S. Clay Court Doubles — Francisco Contreras
U.S. Clay Court Doubles — Alex Olmedo
Canadian Doubles — Earl Baumgardner
NCAA Singles — Alex Olmedo
NCAA Doubles — Alex Olmedo
NCAA Doubles — Francisco Contreras
U.S. Hard Court 18 Singles — Sally Moore
Mexican Doubles — Francisco Contreras

**1957**
U.S. Hard Court Doubles — Alex Olmedo
U.S. Hard Court Mixed Doubles — Sally Moore
U.S. Hard Court Mixed Doubles — Sally Moore
U.S. 18 Doubles — Sally Moore
U.S. Hard Court 18 Singles — Sally Moore
U.S Hard Court 18 Singles — Joe Cowley
Mexican Doubles — Francisco Contreras

**1958**

| | |
|---|---|
| U.S. Doubles | Alex Olmedo |
| U.S. Hard Court Mixed Doubles | Sally Moore |
| Canadian Doubles | Barbara Browning |
| Canadian Doubles | Pamela Davis |
| German Doubles | Francisco Contreras |
| Irish Doubles | Sally Moore |
| Italian Mixed Doubles | Francisco Contreras |
| U.S. Intercollegiate Doubles | Sue Metzger |
| NCAA Singles | Alex Olmedo |
| NCAA Doubles | Alex Olmedo |
| NCAA Doubles | Edward Atkinson |
| NCAA Team Title | USC |
| U.S. 18 Singles | Sally Moore |
| Wimbledon 18 Singles | Sally Moore |
| Mexican Doubles | Francisco Contreras |

**1959**

| | |
|---|---|
| Wimbledon Singles | Alex Olmedo |
| U.S. Indoor Singles | Alex Olmedo |
| U.S. Indoor Doubles | Alex Olmedo |
| Australian Singles | Alex Olmedo |
| Italian Mixed Doubles | Francisco Contreras |
| U.S. Clay Court Singles | Sally Moore |
| U.S. Public Park Singles | Allen Tong |
| U.S. 18 Hard Court Doubles | Barbara Browning |
| U.S. 18 Hard Court Doubles | Pamela Davis |
| U.S. 15 Doubles | Margaret Taylor |
| U.S. 15 Hard Court Doubles | Margaret Taylor |
| U.S. Father and Son Hard Court | Robert Delgado |

**1960**

| | |
|---|---|
| Wimbledon Doubles | Rafael Osuna |
| U.S. Professional Singles | Alex Olmedo |
| U.S. Professional Doubles | Alex Olmedo |
| U.S. 18 Indoor Singles | Sue Behlmar |
| U.S. 18 Indoor Doubles | Sue Behlmar |
| U.S. 15 Doubles | Margaret Taylor |
| U.S. 15 Hard Court Doubles | Margaret Taylor |

**1961**

| | |
|---|---|
| U.S. Doubles | Dennis Ralston |
| U.S. Clay Court Doubles | Dennis Ralston |
| U.S. Hard Court Mixed Doubles | Dick Leach |
| Irish Singles | Bill Bond |
| NCAA Doubles | Rafael Osuna |
| NCAA Doubles | Ramsey Earnhart |
| U.S. Intercollegiate Singles | Tory Fretz (for Occidental College)* |
| U.S. Intercollegiate Doubles | Tory Fretz (for Occidental College)* |
| U.S. Father and Son Hard Court | Bill Bond |
| U.S. Father and Son Grass Court | Bill Bond |

**1962**

| | |
|---|---|
| U.S. Doubles | Rafael Osuna |

---

* Indicates that the championship was won while the individual was attending an institution other than the University of Southern California.

| | |
|---|---|
| U.S. Hard Court Singles | Rafael Osuna |
| U.S. Hard Court Doubles | Rafael Osuna |
| U.S. Clay Court Doubles | Ramsey Earnhart |
| U.S. Hard Court Doubles | Ramsey Earnhart |
| NCAA Singles | Rafael Osuna |
| NCAA Doubles | Rafael Osuna |
| NCAA Doubles | Ramsey Earnhart |
| NCAA Team Title | USC |
| U.S. Intercollegiate Doubles | Linda Yeomans (for Stanford)* |
| | |
| U.S. Father and Son Hard Court | Dennis Ralston |
| U.S. Indoor 18 Singles | Yale Stockwell |
| Central American Games Gold Doubles | Elena Osuna |

**1963**

| | |
|---|---|
| Wimbledon Doubles | Rafael Osuna |
| U.S. Singles | Rafael Osuna |
| U.S. Doubles | Dennis Ralston |
| U.S. Indoor Singles | Dennis Ralston |
| U.S. Indoor Doubles | Dennis Ralston |
| U.S. Hard Court Doubles | Tom Edlefsen |
| U.S. Hard Court Doubles | Bill Bond |
| Mexican Doubles | Rafael Osuna |
| NCAA Singles | Dennis Ralston |
| NCAA Doubles | Dennis Ralston |
| NCAA Doubles | Rafael Osuna |
| NCAA Team Title | USC |
| U.S. Public Parks 18 Doubles | Bob Eisenberg |
| U.S. Father & Son Hardcourt | Bill Bond |
| U.S. Indoor 18 Singles | Yale Stockwell |
| U.S. Indoor 18 Doubles | Yale Stockwell |
| Pan-American Games Gold Mixed Doubles | Francisco Contreras |

**1964**

| | |
|---|---|
| U.S. Clay Court Singles | Dennis Ralston |
| U.S. Clay Court Doubles | Dennis Ralston |
| U.S. Hard Court Singles | Dennis Ralston |
| U.S. Hard Court Doubles | Dennis Ralston |
| U.S. Hardcourt Doubles | Bill Bond |
| U.S. Doubles | Dennis Ralston |
| NCAA Singles | Dennis Ralston |
| NCAA Doubles | Dennis Ralston |
| NCAA Doubles | Bill Bond |
| NCAA Team Title | USC |
| Swiss Singles | Rafael Osuna |
| Mexican Singles | Rafael Osuna |
| Mexican Doubles | Rafael Osuna |
| U.S. Intercollegiate Doubles | Connie Jaster (for UCLA)* |
| | |
| U.S. Public Parks Doubles | Dick Leach |
| U.S. Father and Son Grass | Dennis Ralston |

* Indicates that the championship was won while the individual was attending an institution other than the University of Southern California.

**1965**

| | |
|---|---|
| U.S. Clay Court Singles | Dennis Ralston |
| U.S. Indoor Doubles | Dennis Ralston |
| | |
| U.S. Hard Court Singles | Dennis Ralston |
| U.S. Hard Court Doubles | Dennis Ralston |
| U.S. Hard Court Doubles | Tom Edlefsen |

**1966**

| | |
|---|---|
| Argentine Doubles | Dennis Ralston |
| French Doubles | Dennis Ralston |
| Irish Singles | Jerry Cromwell |
| U.S. Hard Court Singles | Stan Smith |
| U.S. Hard Court Doubles | Stan Smith |
| U.S. Hard Court Doubles | Bob Lutz |
| U.S. Indoor Doubles | Stan Smith |
| U.S. Indoor Doubles | Bob Lutz |
| U.S. Clay Court Doubles | Dennis Ralston |
| Mexican Doubles | Joaquin Loyo-Mayo |
| NCAA Team Title | USC |
| U.S. Intercollegiate Doubles | Yale Stockwell |
| U.S. Father and Son | Bill Bond |
| U.S. Hard Court 16 Doubles | Kris Kemmer |

**1967**

| | |
|---|---|
| U.S. Hard Court Singles | Stan Smith |
| NCAA Doubles | Stan Smith |
| NCAA Doubles | Bob Lutz |
| NCAA Singles | Bob Lutz |
| NCAA Team Title | USC |
| Mexican Doubles | Joaquin Loyo-Mayo |
| U.S. Public Parks 18 Singles | Janie Richardson |
| U.S. Public Parks 18 Doubles | Janie Richardson |
| U.S. 16 Hard Court Doubles | Cindy Thomas |
| U.S. Father and Son Hardcourt | Bill Bond |
| U.S. 16 Singles | Kris Kemmer |

**1968**

| | |
|---|---|
| U.S. Hard Court Singles | Stan Smith |
| British Indoor Mixed Doubles | Stan Smith |
| British Indoor Doubles | Stan Smith |
| British Indoor Doubles | Bob Lutz |
| U.S. Doubles | Stan Smith |
| U.S. Doubles | Bob Lutz |
| U.S. Open Doubles | Stan Smith |
| U.S. Open Doubles | Bob Lutz |
| U.S. Clay Court Doubles | Stan Smith |
| U.S. Clay Court Doubles | Bob Lutz |
| NCAA Singles | Stan Smith |
| NCAA Doubles | Stan Smith |
| NCAA Doubles | Bob Lutz |
| NCAA Team Title | USC |
| U.S. Public Parks 16 Doubles | Molly Tyson |
| Mexican Singles | Joaquin Loyo-Mayo |
| Mexican Doubles | Joaquin Loyo-Mayo |
| Brazilian 18 Singles | Fernando Gentil |
| South American 18 Singles | Fernando Gentil |

| | |
|---|---|
| U.S. Clay Court 18 Doubles | Kris Kemmer |
| U.S. Hard Court 16 Doubles | Kris Kemmer |
| U.S. 16 Doubles | Kris Kemmer |
| U.S. Hard Court Doubles | Rafael Osuna |
| U.S. Hard Court Doubles | Dick Leach |
| U.S. Hard Court Mixed Doubles | Dick Leach |
| U.S. Hard Court 35 Singles | Jacque Grigry |

**1969**

| | |
|---|---|
| U.S. 16 Indoor Doubles | Randy Schneider |
| U.S. Singles | Stan Smith |
| U.S. Indoor Singles | Stan Smith |
| U.S. Indoor Doubles | Stan Smith |
| U.S. Indoor Doubles | Bob Lutz |
| U.S. Hard Court Doubles | Bob Lutz |
| U.S. Hard Court Doubles | Erik van Dillen |
| U.S. Amateur Doubles | Tom Leonard |
| U.S. Amateur Doubles | Erik van Dillen |
| U.S. Amateur Mixed Doubles | Joaquin Loyo-Mayo |
| U.S. 35 Hard Court Singles | Jacque Grigry |
| NCAA Singles | Joaquin Loyo-Mayo |
| NCAA Doubles | Joaquin Loyo-Mayo |
| NCAA Doubles | Marcelo Lara |
| NCAA Team Title | USC |
| U.S. 18 Clay Court Singles | Kris Kemmer |
| U.S. 18 Clay Court Doubles | Kris Kemmer |

**1970**

| | |
|---|---|
| Masters Singles | Stan Smith |
| Masters Doubles | Stan Smith |
| English Indoor Singles | Stan Smith |
| English Indoor Doubles | Stan Smith |
| U.S. Indoor Open Doubles | Stan Smith |
| U.S. Indoor Singles | Stan Smith |
| Australian Doubles | Stan Smith |
| Australian Doubles | Bob Lutz |
| U.S. Indoor Doubles | Stan Smith |
| Mexican Doubles | Joaquin Loyo-Mayo |
| U.S. 18 Doubles | Kris Kemmer |
| U.S. 18 Clay Court Doubles | Kris Kemmer |
| U.S. 14 Doubles | Gretchen Galt |

**1971**

| | |
|---|---|
| U.S. Open Singles | Stan Smith |
| U.S. Hard Court Singles | Bob Lutz |
| Mexican Singles | Joaquin Loyo-Mayo |
| U.S. 16 Indoor Singles | Gretchen Galt |
| U.S. 18 Singles | Raul Ramirez |
| U.S. 18 Hardcourt Singles | Raul Ramirez |
| U.S. 18 Hardcourt Doubles | Raul Ramirez |
| Mexican Doubles | Marcelo Lara |
| Mexican 12 Singles | Mark Novelo |
| Mexican 12 Doubles | Mark Novelo |
| Mexican 18 Singles | Raul Ramirez |
| Mexican 18 Doubles | Raul Ramirez |

**1972**

| | |
|---|---|
| Wimbledon Singles | Stan Smith |
| U.S. Indoor Singles | Stan Smith |
| U.S. Professional Singles | Bob Lutz |
| U.S. Amateur Doubles | Raul Ramirez |
| English Indoor Singles | Stan Smith |
| U.S. Professional Indoor Doubles | Bob Lutz |
| Mexican Doubles | Joaquin Loyo-Mayo |
| U.S. 18 Indoor Doubles | Bruce Manson |
| U.S. 18 Public Parks Doubles | Tim O'Reilly |
| U.S. 16 Doubles | Perry Wright |
| U.S. 16 Doubles | Bruce Manson |
| U.S. 16 Clay Court Doubles | Howard Schoenfield |
| U.S. 16 Hard Court Doubles | Bruce Manson |
| U.S. 16 Hard Court Doubles | Perry Wright |
| U.S. 16 Indoor Singles | Howard Schoenfield |
| U.S. 16 Indoor Doubles | Howard Schoenfield |
| U.S. 16 Indoor Doubles | Perry Wright |

**1973**

| | |
|---|---|
| U.S. Professional Doubles | Stan Smith |
| U.S. Professional Doubles | Erik van Dillen |
| U.S. Professional Indoor Singles | Stan Smith |
| World Championship of Tennis Singles | Stan Smith |
| World Championship of Tennis Doubles | Stan Smith |
| World Championship of Tennis Doubles | Bob Lutz |
| Belgian Professional Singles | Stan Smith |
| Belgian Professional Doubles | Stan Smith |
| Belgian Professional Doubles | Bob Lutz |
| German Professional Singles | Stan Smith |
| Indian Doubles | Raul Ramirez |
| Mexican Singles | Joaquin Loyo-Mayo |
| Mexican Doubles | Joaquin Loyo-Mayo |
| Mexican Doubles | Marcelo Lara |
| South African Professional Doubles | Bob Lutz |
| South African Professional Doubles | Stan Smith |
| Swedish Open Singles | Stan Smith |
| Swedish Open Doubles | Stan Smith |
| U.S. 18 Indoor Singles | Howard Schoenfield |
| U.S. 18 Indoor Doubles | Howard Schoenfield |
| U.S. 16 Clay Court Singles | Howard Schoenfield |

**1974**

| | |
|---|---|
| U.S. Doubles | Bob Lutz |
| U.S. Doubles | Stan Smith |
| U.S. Professional Doubles | Bob Lutz |
| U.S. Professional Doubles | Stan Smith |
| Australian Indoor Singles | Stan Smith |
| Italian Doubles | Raul Ramirez |
| Mexican Doubles | Joaquin Loyo-Mayo |
| U.S. Public Parks Doubles | Hillary Hilton |
| U.S. Public Parks Mixed Doubles | Hillary Hilton |
| U.S. 18 Public Parks Doubles | Carlos Hassey |
| U.S. 18 Hard Court Doubles | Bruce Manson |
| U.S. 18 Hard Court Doubles | Perry Wright |
| U.S. 18 Clay Court Doubles | Bruce Manson |
| U.S. 18 Clay Court Doubles | Perry Wright |
| U.S. Father and Son Hardcourt | Butch Walts |

# APPENDIX

**1975**

| | |
|---|---|
| U.S. Professional Doubles | Raul Ramirez |
| World Championship of Tennis Doubles | Raul Ramirez |
| Australian Indoor Singles | Stan Smith |
| French Open Doubles | Raul Ramirez |
| Italian Singles | Raul Ramirez |
| Italian Doubles | Raul Ramirez |
| Japan Open Singles | Raul Ramirez |
| Japan Open Doubles | Raul Ramirez |
| Mexican Singles | Joaquin Loyo-Mayo |
| Mexican Doubles | Joaquin Loyo-Mayo |
| Mexican Doubles | Marcelo Lara |
| U.S. Clay Court Amateur Doubles | Butch Walts |
| U.S. Clay Court Amateur Doubles | Diane Desfor |
| U.S. Public Parks Doubles | Hillary Hilton |
| NCAA Doubles | Butch Walts |
| NCAA Doubles | Bruce Manson |
| Pan-Am Games Doubles | Bruce Manson |
| Pan-Am Games Doubles | Butch Walts |
| U.S. 18 Singles | Howard Schoenfield |
| U.S. 18 Hard Court Singles | Howard Schoenfield |
| U.S. Open Junior Boys Singles | Howard Schoenfield |

**1976**

| | |
|---|---|
| Wimbledon Doubles | Raul Ramirez |
| U.S. Clay Court Doubles | Raul Ramirez |
| U.S. Professional Indoor Doubles | Dennis Ralston |
| Canadian Doubles | Raul Ramirez |
| Grand Prix Singles | Raul Ramirez |
| Grand Prix Doubles | Raul Ramirez |
| Italian Doubles | Raul Ramirez |
| Spanish Doubles | Raul Ramirez |
| Swiss Singles | Raul Ramirez |
| U.S. Amateur Grass Court Singles | Chris Lewis |
| U.S. Amateur Grass Court Mixed Doubles | Chris Lewis |
| U.S. Amateur Grass Court Mixed Doubles | Cindy Thomas |
| U.S. Amateur Grass Court Singles | Diane Desfor |
| U.S. 18 Hard Court Singles | Robert Van't Hof |
| U.S. Public Parks Doubles | Hillary Hilton |
| U.S. 21 Singles | Bruce Manson |
| U.S. 21 Doubles | Chris Lewis |
| U.S. 21 Doubles | Gretchen Galt |
| U.S. 35 Indoor Doubles | Horst Ritter |
| U.S. 35 Indoor Doubles | Dick Leach |
| U.S. 35 Indoor Singles | Horst Ritter |

**1977**

| | |
|---|---|
| U.S. Professional Indoor Doubles | Stan Smith |
| U.S. Professional Indoor Doubles | Bob Lutz |
| Canadian Doubles | Raul Ramirez |
| French Doubles | Raul Ramirez |
| Italian Doubles | Raul Ramirez |
| Mexican Doubles | Joaquin Loyo-Mayo |
| South Africa Open Doubles | Bob Lutz |
| South Africa Open Doubles | Stan Smith |
| U.S. Amateur Indoor Doubles | Perry Wright |
| NCAA Doubles | Chris Lewis |

| | |
|---|---|
| NCAA Doubles | Bruce Manson |
| U.S. 21 Indoor Doubles | Bruce Manson |
| U.S. 21 Singles | Bruce Manson |

**1978**

| | |
|---|---|
| U.S. Open Doubles | Bob Lutz |
| U.S. Open Doubles | Stan Smith |
| U.S. Indoor Doubles | Raul Ramirez |
| U.S. Amateur Indoor Singles | Robert Van't Hof |
| U.S. Amateur Clay Court Doubles | Doug Adler |
| Mexican Open Singles | Raul Ramirez |
| U.S. 21 Indoor Singles | Robert Van't Hof |
| U.S. 21 Indoor Doubles | Robert Van't Hof |
| U.S. 21 Indoor Doubles | Glen Petrovic |
| Central American Games Gold Doubles | Alejandra Vallejo |

**1979**

| | |
|---|---|
| Italian Indoor Open Singles | Butch Walts |
| Spanish Singles | Hans Gildemeister |
| U.S. Father and Son Hardcourt | Dick Leach |
| U.S. 21 Doubles | Robert Van't Hof |
| U.S. 21 Hard Court Doubles | Robert Van't Hof |
| U.S. 45 Hard Court Singles | Jim Perley |

**1980**

| | |
|---|---|
| U.S. Open Doubles | Bob Lutz |
| U.S. Open Doubles | Stan Smith |
| World Championship of Tennis Doubles | Raul Ramirez |
| Italian Indoor Doubles | Butch Walts |
| NCAA Singles | Robert Van't Hof |
| U.S. Amateur Indoor Doubles | Jack Kruger |
| U.S. Amateur Indoor Doubles | Sean Brawley |
| U.S. Father and Son Clay Court | Dick Leach |
| Canadian Doubles | Bruce Manson |
| South African Doubles | Stan Smith |
| South African Doubles | Bob Lutz |
| Mexican Doubles | Alejandra Vallejo |
| Mexican Doubles | Jorge Lozano |
| Mexican Doubles | Rafael Belmar Osuna |
| U.S. Indoor 18 Doubles | Jorge Lozano |
| U.S. Indoor Amateur Singles | Roger Knapp |
| Casablanca International Doubles | Jorge Lozano |
| Casablanca International Doubles | Rafael Belmar Osuna |

**1981**

| | |
|---|---|
| U.S. Amateur Clay Court Mixed | Jim Agate |
| U.S. Amateur Indoor Doubles | Jim Agate |
| U.S. Public Parks Doubles | Doug Adler |
| U.S. Public Parks Mixed | Doug Adler |
| U.S. 40 Hard Court Doubles | Sally Moore Huss |
| U.S. 40 Grass Court Singles | Horst Ritter |
| U.S. Father and Son Hardcourt | Dick Leach |
| US Interscholastic Team Championships Doubles | Jorge Lozano |
| US Interscholastic Team Championships Doubles | Rafael Belmar Osuna |
| Canadian Doubles | Raul Ramirez |
| U.S. Public Parks Doubles | Mike Margolin |
| Mexican Doubles | Claudia Hernandez |

| | |
|---|---|
| Mexican Doubles | Jorge Lozano |
| Mexican Doubles | Rafael Belmar Osuna |
| Rolex International Doubles | Jorge Lozano |
| Rolex International Doubles | Rafael Belmar Osuna |
| Casablanca International Doubles | Jorge Lozano |
| Casablanca International Doubles | Rafael Belmar Osuna |

**1982**

| | |
|---|---|
| U.S. 45 Hard Court Singles | Jim Perley |
| U.S. 40-45 Hard Court Mixed | Sally Moore Huss |
| U.S. Father and Son Hardcourt | Butch Walts |
| U.S. Hard Court 45 Doubles | Penny Stewart |
| Central America & Caribbean Singles | Claudia Hernandez |
| Orange Bowl 16 Singles | Claudia Hernandez |
| Mexican Singles | Claudia Hernandez |
| Mexican Doubles | Claudia Hernandez |
| Mexican 18 & Under Doubles | Rafael Belmar Osuna |

**1983**

| | |
|---|---|
| U.S. 40 Grass Court Singles | Dick Leach |
| U.S. 45 Hard Court Singles | Les Dodson |
| U.S. Father and Son Hardcourt | Dick Leach |
| Mexican Doubles | Claudia Hernandez |

**1984**

| | |
|---|---|
| U.S. 40 Hardcourt Singles | Sally Moore Huss |
| U.S. 40 Hardcourt Doubles | Sally Moore Huss |
| U.S. 45 Indoor Singles | Les Dodson |
| U.S. 50 Grass Court Singles | Jim Perley |
| Masters Singles | Stan Smith |
| Mexican Singles | Claudia Hernandez |

**1985**

| | |
|---|---|
| U.S. 40 Clay Court Singles | Sally Moore Huss |
| U.S. 40 Clay Court Doubles | Sally Moore Huss |
| U.S. 45 Hard Court Doubles | Dick Leach |
| U.S. Father and Son Clay Court | Dick Leach |
| U.S. Father and Son Grass Court | Dick Leach |
| Masters Singles | Bob Lutz |
| Masters 35 Doubles | Bob Lutz |
| Masters 35 Doubles | Stan Smith |
| Junior International 18 Doubles | Lupita Novelo |
| Mexican Singles | Claudia Hernandez |
| Mexican Doubles | Claudia Hernandez |
| Mexican Father & Son Doubles | Francisco Contreras |

**1986**

| | |
|---|---|
| U.S. Clay Court Doubles | Hans Gildemeister |
| U.S. 35 Hard Court Doubles | Sally Moore Huss |
| U.S. 40 Hard Court Doubles | Sally Moore Huss |
| U.S. 45 Hard Court Singles | Sally Moore Huss |
| U.S. 45 Hard Court Singles | Gordon Davis |
| U.S. 45 Indoor Doubles | Les Dodson |
| U.S. 45 Grass Court Doubles | Les Dodson |
| U.S. 50 Hard Court Singles | Jim Perley |
| Mexican Singles | Jorge Lozano |
| Mexican Singles | Claudia Hernandez |

Mexican Doubles — Claudia Hernandez

**1987**
U.S. 45 Hard Court Doubles — Sally Moore Huss
U.S. 45 Indoor Doubles — Les Dodson
U.S. Father and Son Hardcourt — Dick Leach
Mexican Singles — Claudia Hernandez
Mexican Father & Son Doubles — Rafael Belmar Osuna

**1988**
U.S. 50 Indoor Singles — Les Dodson
U.S. 50 Grass Court Doubles — Gordon Davis
U.S. 55 Indoor Singles — Jim Perley
French Mixed Doubles — Jorge Lozano
Mexican Singles — Claudia Hernandez

**1989**
U.S. 50 Grass Court Singles — Gordon Davis
U.S. Father and Son Hard Court — Dick Leach
Mexican Singles — Claudia Hernandez
Mexican Doubles — Alejandra Vallejo

**1990**
U.S. 55 Grass Court Singles — Gordon Davis
U.S. Grass Court 30 Doubles — Gordon Davis
U.S. 55 Hard Court Singles — Gordon Davis
U.S. Father and Son Grass Court — Dick Leach
U.S. 50 Hard Court Singles — Alex Olmedo
French Mixed Doubles — Jorge Lozano

**1991**
U.S. Father and Son Grass Court — Dick Leach

**1992**
U.S. 55 Singles Hard Court — Alex Olmedo
U.S. Father and Son Hardcourt — Dick Leach
Mexican Doubles — Jorge Lozano

**1993**
U.S. 55 Singles Hard Court — Alex Olmedo
U.S. Father and Son Hard Court — Dick Leach
Mexican Doubles — Alejandra Vallejo

**1994**
U.S. Father and Son Hard Court — Dick Leach

**1995**
U.S. 55 Hard Court Doubles — Dick Leach

**1996**
U.S. Father and Son Hard Court — Dick Leach

**2006**
Mexican Doubles — Alejandra Vallejo

# TOLEY NATIONAL OR INTERNATIONAL CHAMPIONS
## 77 athletes — 460 titles — 10 USC team titles

1. Doug Adler [3 titles]
2. Jim Agate [2 titles
3. Ed Atkinson [2 titles]
4. Earl Baumgardner [4 titles]
5. Sue Behlmar [2 titles]
6. Rafael Belmar Osuna [7 titles]
7. Bill Bond [9 titles]
8. Sean Brawley [1 title]
9. Barbara Browning [2 titles]
10. Allen Call [1 title]
11. Allen Cleveland [2 titles]
12. Francisco Contreras [11 titles]
13. Joe Cowley [2 titles]
14. Jerry Cromwell [1 title]
15. Gordon Davis [6 titles]
16. Pamela Davis [2 titles]
17. Robert Delgado [1 title]
18. Diane Desor [2 titles]
19. Les Dodson [6 titles]
20. Nancy Dwyer [2 titles]
21. Ramsey Earnhart [4 titles]
22. Tom Edlefsen [2 titles]
23. Bob Eisenberg [2 titles]
24. Tory Fretz [2 titles]
25. Gretchen Galt [3 titles]
26. Fernando Gentil [2 titles]
27. Hans Gildemeister [2 titles]
28. Brooke Grant [1 title]
29. Gregory Grant [3 titles]
30. Jacque Grigry [2 titles]
31. Carlos Hassey [1 title]
32. Claudia Hernandez [14 titles]
33. Hillary Hilton [4 titles]
34. Connie Jaster [1 title]
35. Kris Kemmer [9 titles]
36. Roger Knapp [1 title]
37. Jack Kruger [1 title]
38. Marcelo Lara [4 titles]
39. Dick Leach [22 titles]
40. Tom Leonard [1 title]
41. Chris Lewis [4 titles]
42. Joaquin Loyo-Mayo [14 titles]
43. Jorge Lozano [11 titles]
44. Bob Lutz [27 titles]
45. Bruce Manson [12 titles]
46. Mike Margolin [1 title]
47. Sue Metzger [1 title]
48. Sally Moore (later Huss) [21 titles]
49. Lupita Novelo [1 title]
50. Mark Novelo [2 titles]
51. Alex Olmedo [17 titles]
52. Tim O'Reilly [1 title]
53. Elena Osuna [1 title]
54. Rafael Osuna [19 titles]
55. Jim Perley [5 titles]
56. Glen Petrovic [1 title]
57. Dennis Ralston [24 titles]
58. Raul Ramirez [29 titles]
59. Joaquin Reyes [1 title]
60. Janie Richardson [2 titles]
61. Horst Ritter [3 titles]
62. Julie Sampson [5 titles]
63. Randy Schneider [1 title]
64. Howard Schoenfield [9 titles]
65. Stan Smith [49 titles]
66. Penny Stewart [1 title]
67. Yale Stockwell [4 titles]
68. Margaret Taylor [4 titles]
69. Cindy Thomas [2 titles]
70. Allen Tong [1 title]
71. Molly Tyson [1 title]
72. Erik van Dillen [3 titles]
73. Alejandra Vallejo [6 titles]
74. Robert Van't Hof [7 titles]
75. Butch Walts [7 titles]
76. Perry Wright [6 titles]
77. Linda Yeomans [1 title]

# TOLEY'S RATING OF TENNIS WEAPONS

*Best Forehand*

That would be Elly Vines, with Jack Kramer, John Newcombe and Ivan Lendl also very good.

Vines played the game differently than anybody else has ever played it that I know of, in that every ball he hit he just went for a winner. Every ball. And when he was on, of course, he was fantastic, but he couldn't be on all the time. People at the L.A. Tennis Club wouldn't play with him, because he'd hit the ball into the fence or hit a winner, so his opponent didn't get any practice. He was a fence-buster in his younger days, but then all of a sudden everything jelled. Someone asked what his theory was in tennis, his strategy. He said, ``Well, first ball I try to hit in the corner for a winner. If it comes back, I try to hit it in the other corner for a winner. If it comes back, I'll hit the third ball for a winner if I can.''

Best at USC: Raul Ramirez might go in that category. He had a fine forehand with topspin, and he was consistent, could do lots of things with it.

*Best Backhand*

Don Budge. He played the ball on the rise, first of all, and he had consistency. And it was forceful. Every ball Budge hit was a heavy ball. He didn't swing hard, but the ball came off the racket with pace. With his 17-ounce racket, he didn't use the slice backhand that often. He went right over the top of the ball – slight topspin is what it was.

Best at USC: Dennis Ralston.

*Best Forehand Volley*

Jack Kramer had a forehand volley that was so tough. He got it a foot from the baseline, or on the baseline, practically every time. That was his aim. He never volleyed short.

Now Pancho Gonzalez, his volleys were not as tough, but you couldn't pass him. That's one of the main reasons he was a great player, because you couldn't pass him at the net. But he never volleyed forcefully, aggressively like Jack did.

Best at USC: Close between Ralston and Alex Olmedo. Ralston was a little more forceful; Alex might have been a little more consistent, maybe safer, but he got that way because he didn't put as much on it. So I think Denny perhaps.

*Best Backhand Volley*

Tony Roche, the Australian left-hander, had an awfully good one. I think what made it so good was that it was a short punch. It wasn't a big swing, and he had great touch on the thing. Whenever the subject comes up with players, they usually say it was Roche on the backhand volley.

Best at USC: Stan Smith.

*Best Half-Volley*

Don Budge, by far. He was such a good half-volleyer that when he played doubles he never charged the net. He just walked in there. When he was caught in no-man's land, between the net and the baseline, it didn't bother him at all.

Best at USC: Ralston.

*Best First Serve*

There was a big left-hander who won the nationals only because of his serve: Johnny Doeg. He beat Francis X. Shields in 1930 and all he had on both sides was a chip. So he was barely adequate, except for his serve. He could serve four aces in a row. The ball favored the server then. It was very light, easy to hit hard. He was accurate and could spin it like mad – tremendous spin. Had a big hook on the thing.

**194**

One story I heard, they were playing the finals in national doubles. Doeg won it twice with George Lott Jr.,in 1929 and 1930, and it got to be like 12-10 in the fifth or something like that. They finally broke serve and had to serve for the match, and Doeg said, ``Give me those God-damned balls,' and served four aces in a row.

Best at USC: Stan Smith. He had that 6-3 height. In crucial parts of a match when he really had to get that first one in, his chances of doing it were pretty good.

### Best Second Serve
I'll take Jack Kramer's, because it was so forceful. It was the toughest second serve to return.

Gonzalez's second serve I wouldn't put in the top 50. He just spun it in; it was nothing super. I was a linesman on his matches and he was great for a linesman because the ball was some distance from the back line all the time!

But Gonzalez moved so well, he didn't think it was worth the gamble to hit that deep. Kramer didn't move as well as Gonzalez, so he depended on a tough, deep second serve, and he would serve a lot of double faults on occasion. He was in the final of the Southern Cal one year and in one game he must have served six double faults and still won.

Pete Sampras is a contender here because he served aces often on his second serve. Kramer didn't gamble that much on it; he had heavy spin on the ball that made it tough to handle, but it wasn't the type of serve that was apt to ace you.

Best at USC: Smith.

### Best Return of Serve
Don Budge. His return was tougher than Jimmy Connors'.

Best at USC: Ralston. He took it on the rise.

### Best Passing Shots
Budge again, because he stopped Kramer from coming into the net, on grass, and that's amazing considering Jack's big serve and big volley. He made Jack stay back.

Best at USC: Ralston. He played the ball on the rise and was good off the ground.

### Best Overhead
It's hard to choose among Gonzalez, Kramer and Pete Sampras. They all had exceptional overheads. Just didn't miss.

Best at USC: You can't choose among Olmedo, Smith and Ralston. They all had good overheads.

### Best Lob
Bobby Riggs. I don't know if anybody else was really outstanding, but one match sticks in my mind. Rafael Osuna played the Spaniard, Manuel Santana, at Wimbledon – I think the quarters in 1965, the year Santana won it. Rafe won the first two sets and 0 and 1, and Santana was out of the match, or so it seemed. So he just started hitting topspin lobs off both sides. He killed Rafe with topspin lobs and won the match.

Best at USC: Osuna and Ralston. Denny played the ball on the rise more than the rest of the guys did, so that made him more aggressive and more apt to have success with his lobs.

### Best Touch
Bobby Riggs probably had the best. His whole game was touch. He sliced a lot, he drop-volleyed a lot and had great feel.

### Best Footwork and Court Coverage

Overall, it would be Pancho Gonzalez. He was dominating at the net and in the backcourt he moved well, and he had that large size, which was a big advantage. I don't see how you could get much better than Gonzalez.

There's another guy I might put in there, too, maybe put him No. 1: Fred Perry. I watched him play and I never can remember him having to scramble. Eyes are a big factor. Some people have a knack of just before the ball is hit, they know exactly where it's going to go. That person might not be so fast, but he covers because of that factor.

Best at USC: Osuna by far. He had so much speed on the court, that's how he won.

### Best Right-side Doubles

Definitely John Bromwich of Australia, who won so much with countryman Adrian Quist, and won the U.S. nationals with Quist, William Sidwell and Frank Sedgman. He won the Australian with Quist eight times, and Wimbledon twice, with Quist and Sedgman. He won 13 Wimbledons and Australians and our nationals with different partners, and he won some of them way past his prime.

Usually the right-side guy is the steadier partner, because you can't make as many plays there. But Bromwich controlled the match from the deuce court, because he hit tremendous angles.

I played against him in the national doubles and really, I didn't know whether I'd rather serve or have him serve. Because if I served, he was just killing me. He'd just flick his return and it was always down at my feet.

Best at USC: Ralston.

### Best Left-side Doubles

Don Budge.

Best at USC: Osuna.

### Best Strategy

Bobby Riggs knew what to do. Bobby could do so many things on a tennis court, and they were always the right things. He couldn't beat you with outright power, but he could do everything else there was in winning a match. For instance, if you were at the net, he knew just how far you could go to get to his shot, and he'd pass you and hit five feet inside the sideline, because he knew that was enough. That was the kind of mind Bobby had. Bobby would find a way to win. He was a great competitor.

A vital bit of strategy is: Forget Your Mistakes. There are certain people who can miss a shot and then approach the next one as if nothing had happened. It's a great gift to have, and that's the kind of mind Ellsworth Vines had. At match point, he was famous for knocking off winners. People of high caliber, their mistakes don't bother them.

The best example I can give you is Jack Kramer in the final at Forest Hills against Frank Parker in 1947. He had always beaten Parker, but he was having a bad day and Parker won the first two sets. Kramer was missing the lines time and time again. But he never changed one iota, because in his mind he knew he'd get going and then the match would be over. About the third game of the third set, he started clicking and the match was over. Kramer won 4-6, 2-6, 6-1, 6-0, 6-3. It was a real important match, too, because Kramer was about to turn pro and if he lost that final, he wouldn't have gotten the contract. His whole future rested on that match.

# INDEX

## ABOUT CO-AUTHOR
## JOE JARES

Joe Jares began developing his journalist's credentials at an early age. He was first a reporter, then editor of his high school's weekly newspaper. At the University of Southern California, Joe served as sports editor and managing editor of the *Daily Trojan*.

After his 1959 graduation, he served on the staffs of the *Los Angeles Herald-Express*, UPI, the *Los Angeles Times*, *Sports Illustrated* and the *Los Angeles Daily News*.

He has taught journalism classes for many years at USC and is the author of seven previous books, including *Whatever Happened to Gorgeous George?*, a humorous book about pro wrestling. *Sports Illustrated* named it one of the 100 best sports books of all time.

Joe wrote a feature for *Sports Illustrated* about George Toley in 1975. This led to a long friendship with the famed tennis coach and the collaboration that led to this book.